WORLD-CLASS

SPEED

THE PROVEN KPI-BASED STRUCTURE
TO ACCELERATE BUSINESS GROWTH

By Peter C. Fuller

EXPERTISE
PUBLISHING

Published by: Expertise Publishing
ExpertisePublishing.com

Paperback ISBN: 979-8-9907448-0-6
Hardcover ISBN: 979-8-9907448-1-3
eBook ISBN: 979-8-9907448-2-0
Library of Congress Control Number: 2024911278

Publisher: Expertise Publishing – ExpertisePublishing.com
Interior Design: Noelle Peterson

Connect with Peter Fuller at LinkedIn.com/in/petercfuller

ENDORSEMENTS

"Fuller has figured it out! You want to run your business, but it feels like it's running you. 'World-Class Speed' will show you how to put together the plan, processes, and people so you can own your life and your business. 'World-Class Speed' is jet fuel to achieve world-class faster and better."

Daniel Lieberman
CEO - Valuable Leadership

"'World-Class Speed' lives up to its title – it is a quick read. But quick does not mean shallow. This is one of those rare business books that lends itself to multiple re-reads. There is a lot of business wisdom here to unpack – especially when it comes to the importance of KPIs to align everyone in a business and hold folks accountable for their results. The book also makes a strong case for starting the development of your business by starting with yourself and ensuring that your business supports your personal and professional goals. Written in a breezy, concise style 'World-Class Speed' delivers on its title, especially with its take on how to make meetings work – fast!!

A highly recommended read for anyone who is a business owner or executive."

Geoff Hetherington The Profitability Coach
Founder - The Elite Business Institute

"'World-Class Speed' underscores the importance of accountability in any successful business. Clear targets and proper accountability make individuals' performance measurable, allowing them to self-reflect. By implementing this philosophy in our businesses, we will create an environment where every team member understands their role and contributes effectively towards our shared goals."

Jack Findley
CEO - Sterling Signal Firm

"Peter Fuller is a fantastic KPI expert, speaker, and teacher. We had him speak to our Vistage group of CEOs and he kept their rapt attention the entire afternoon. If you need to understand how to use KPIs, OKRs or other metrics to manage a business, or business unit, Peter Fuller is the person to turn to for insights and advice."

Walter Paulsen
Vistage Chair

"In 'World-Class Speed,' Peter Fuller critically examines existing operating models, specifically their handling of Key Performance Indicators (KPIs). While various models touch upon KPIs, they frequently fall short in positioning them effectively to drive the essential actions for achieving desired results. Fuller contends that addressing gaps or deltas – the disparities between current performance and desired outcomes – is pivotal for making informed decisions and propelling a company toward World-Class status, all at a greater speed than typically observed."

David Leavitt
CEO - CXO Advisory, LLC

"Once again, Peter Fuller challenges conventional wisdom by telling entrepreneurs to reclaim the precious resource of time to thrive in business and life. 'World-Class Speed' empowers readers to build world-class companies by redefining success metrics and deploying powerful principles that lead to sustainable professional and personal growth."

Nathalie Duval-Couetil, Ph.D.
Purdue University Krannert School of Management.

"'World-Class Speed' is an excellent resource that helps guide companies regarding what they need to do to become world-class. I highly recommend this 'must-read' book."

Mark Iwanowski, NFL Player
Former Managing Director - Trident Capital

"Game changer. 'World-Class Speed'—the title says it all! Peter cuts through the noise flooding today's business market. Fully implemented, these simple steps guarantee exceptional results in record time!"

Jerry Howard
Founder - iNTREPiD iMPACT Team

"I was able to align my team, reduce time spent in meetings, focus on myself and grow my business simultaneously. I couldn't have done that without Catipult."

Diana Stewart
CEO - Envirox

"At last, a clear roadmap empowering leaders to transition from working "in" the business to working "on" the business. In 'World-Class Speed,' Peter Fuller unveils a transformative mindset, starting with you as the leader, swiftly propelling your company to World-Class status with accelerated growth, profitability, and valuation. Peter Fuller's 'World-Class Speed' is a turbocharged roadmap to business and personal success. Get ready to accelerate your business and transform your life."

Gary Rosenstein
CEO, Board Chair, Certified Catipult Coach

"I've tried many systems and there is nothing that compares to Catipult. It's incredibly simple to understand, highly focused and elevates personal wellbeing as a business success factor."

Derrick Christy
CEO - Approved Mortgage

"This is the next generation of operating systems. Its combination of valuation driving metrics and structure is a game changer."

Tom Morgan
Master Vistage Chair

"This structure allowed me to double my business and align my team. I couldn't have done it without it and I wouldn't consider managing my company without Catipult."

Ken Thieneman
CEO - Thieneman Construction

TABLE OF CONTENTS

Endorsements   iii

Foreword   ix

Introduction   xi

Chapter 1: Jets and World-Class   1

Chapter 2: The Components of a World-Class Company and Process   9

Chapter 3: Start with You   21

Chapter 4: The Outcome Statement   53

Chapter 5: Mission, Vision, and Values   63

Chapter 6: Focused, World-Class KPI Targets   71

Chapter 7: Action Items: Related to KPIs   101

Chapter 8: Faster Meetings, Better Results   113

Chapter 9: People   153

Chapter 10: Catipult Coaching - the Glue Between Immutable KPIs and

        Meeting Excellence   167

Industry Expert Interviews and Case Studies: 177

Gratitude and Acknowledgements   193

Glossary   195

Endnotes   199

About the Author   201

Catipult AI   203

FOREWORD

By Brandon Barnum – CEO of HOA.com

In the fast-paced world of business, speed is not just an advantage; it's a necessity. However, speed without structure can lead to chaos, inefficiency, and burnout.

This is where Peter Fuller's book, *World-Class Speed: The Proven KPI-Based Structure to Accelerate Business Growth* comes into play. This book is not just a guide; it's a roadmap to reclaiming control over your business and your life. It's a comprehensive system for success.

If you've ever felt like your business is running you instead of you running your business, this book is your solution. '*World-Class Speed*' will show you how to create a cohesive plan, refine your processes, and build a strong, motivated team so you can reclaim control of your business and your life. It's the jet fuel that propels you to achieve world-class results faster and better, allowing you to reach your goals with unprecedented efficiency.

The strategies outlined in this book will not only help you streamline your operations, but also create a positive and productive work environment.

That's because, this book underscores the importance of starting with the "You Driver" which is unique to each person on your team.

Your business should be a vehicle that supports your personal and professional aspirations, not the other way around. This principle is woven throughout the book, offering a holistic approach to business growth. Ensuring that your business supports your personal and professional goals is crucial, and '*World-Class Speed*' provides the framework to achieve this balance.

The emphasis on Key Performance Indicators (KPIs) is particularly powerful. KPIs are more than just metrics; they are the foundation for aligning your team, setting clear expectations, and holding everyone accountable.

When you combine the strategies in this book with the Catipult AI software platform, you have a powerful way to organize your business and team to be more effective and efficient, providing a clear path to operational excellence.

Catipult AI puts the principles in this book into action giving you a metrics-based customized plan for everyone on your team to help you succeed faster. The metrics it generates will help increase your valuation, improve employee retention, and create better team alignment.

That's why we've chosen to use the Catipult AI system to manage our companies. The Catipult AI dashboard keeps KPIs for our seven business drivers front and center so everyone on the team is focused on delivering results. This drives consistent and measurable growth, ensuring that your business is always moving in the right direction.

'*World-Class Speed*' is a must-read for any business leader aiming to accelerate growth without compromising quality or personal well-being. It's a treasure trove of business wisdom, offering a proven KPI-based structure that, combined with the innovative capabilities of Catipult AI, helps you outpace the competition.

Prepare to be inspired, enlightened, and equipped to take your business to unprecedented heights. Whether you are a seasoned entrepreneur or just starting out, this book will provide you with the tools and strategies you need to succeed in today's fast-paced business world.

Brandon Barnum
CEO of HOA.com

INTRODUCTION

INDIANAPOLIS: Curt, the CEO of Endangered Species Chocolate, purchased a cabin in Michigan, but spending four contiguous weeks there with his family was only a dream. His family often went without him. Instead, his presence was often required back at the office. As his children aged, the issue of not spending this quality time with them became acute.

MILWAUKEE: Robert the CEO of a machine manufacturing company, was beginning to drink a bit more than usual when he returned home from work. His sleep was deteriorating, and his health problems were increasing. As a third-generation owner, one Key Performance Indicator (KPI) was haunting him: his concentration of revenue from one customer was at 80 percent.

NEW YORK CITY: Jennifer, a successful CEO on Madison Avenue, always wanted to be a yoga instructor but she never found the time to do it while running her companies. This desire weighed on her into her late fifties. Like drip torture, it never went away and began impacting her drive. She also had another issue that was brushed aside for too long: her concentration of revenue from one customer had grown from 20 percent to 70 percent in just 18 months.

ATLANTA: Melissa was the CEO of a very successful training company she had built and run for more than 30 years. Revenues had flattened over the years and nothing they seemed to do was able to boost growth rates. The problem wasn't with the product, it was with one metric: churn. They had no idea how much revenue was leaving annually, as they only measured churn by new customers coming in against old customers leaving.

WESTFIELD, Indiana: Ken was determined to grow his company to $100 million. At $65 million, the company was stalled. According to their KPIs, they needed $140 million in the pipeline and their sales team reported $550 million. Despite exceeding the pipeline by five times, growth was elusive. The reason: their pipeline calculation was inaccurate. They needed $1.1 billion in the project pipeline to achieve $100 million in revenue.

LOS ANGELES: Kevin was the CEO of a company that provided storage solutions to large warehouses. After nearly 30 years in business, he was ready to sell the company back to his employees for $100 million. As with any Employee Stock Option Plan (ESOP), a bank needs to back it. After a careful review, the bank shaved $35 million off the valuation and told him to go back and fix one key metric: his revenue concentration in one customer. He lost three years of his retirement correcting this issue.

SILICON VALLEY: Simon is the CEO of a tech company in the data storage and networking space. The company had developed a significant piece of technology that could outperform most of its competitors. The key challenge: One competitor dominated the space with 95 percent market share and was the de facto standard. Nevertheless, Simon built a strategy that promised billions in revenue … but that never materialized. The reason: their metrics were way off as they miscalculated their total addressable market. Rather than billions, it was less than a billion. Mathematically, the maximum revenue the company could achieve with their current strategy was around $55 million. Eight years after pursuing the strategy, the company was at $60 million in annual revenue and had raised $225 million to get there.

Stories Like These Could Fill An Entire Book

The pressures of running a business are great and scenarios like those above can lead to all sorts of bad habits. In fact, as a class, business owners have the highest rates of divorce, suicide, drug addiction, bankruptcy, and alcoholism. We work hard and die fast in the pursuit of freedom.

I've seen and experienced the good, the bad and the ugly of business ownership. Personally, I'm divorced and have been very close to bankruptcy more than once. I've raised money, sold companies, lost money, and missed far too much of my children's life in pursuit of the freedom to spend more time with them.

I've coached the loneliest of people—business owners and CEOs. Many have cried during one-on-ones, struggling to be a good parent and good employer and failing—in their mind—at both. I've worked with CEOs going through divorce and those who needed to self-medicate before they came home each night so they could be present with the family and remove, if just for a few hours, the stress of business.

As owners, we're a weird and rare bunch. We desire freedom so much and the ability to pursue a vision, that we'll push through obstacles most people will never face. Employees who steal hundreds of thousands from us, fake allegations designed to extort settlements, spouses who just "don't get it," and living with cash shortages when customers are late on payments, and much more.

Yet, we press on. Why? Because it's worth it. The pursuit of a vision—whatever that may be—is the ultimate expression of freedom. It's not surprising then that the image of a private jet is the most common metaphor for ultimate success among the owners I've interviewed, even though it comes dead last in the list of success metrics they have for themselves (as it should).

Ahead of the jet comes a strong desire to build a legacy of doing good for the community, starting or contributing to charities, and building generational wealth for their families. The best entrepreneurs also want to take care of their employees and make sure that the ones who gifted them with their loyalty are rewarded greatly. For the owners I've interviewed, possessing a jet simply means you've taken care of the priorities that really matter, first.

So Why The Jet As A Metaphor For This Book?

A jet is speed. A jet is freedom. A jet is a world-class machine that operates flawlessly at high speeds, giving whoever is riding the ultimate gift—more time back. And that's what we all want. Speed, freedom, a world-class operation, and more time back to build that legacy, contribute our time and resources to charities, and spend time with family.

It's very hard to have it all and be it all.

It doesn't have to be, and this book will show you how to do it all in less time, with less stress and greater results.

Personally, I've started to feed the homeless every Wednesday from 11 a.m. - 1 p.m. at the local church within walking distance from me. Until coming up with this process, it would have been very hard for me to take time off in the middle of the day and in the middle of the week. I'm spending more time with family and doing the things that I value because I have more time back.

And that's what I want for you. Time. Back.

And so, after months of thinking, the answer to the question "to whom should this book be dedicated" became obvious: you. You're in the 3.8 percent of the world's population who dare to employ others. You're in an elite class. Most small businesses fail in the first three years, only 6.9 percent succeed after three years, and only 1.7 percent succeed after ten.[1] The principles and structure you'll find in this book are simple to execute and will give you a world-class company so you can live a life of freedom.

Let's get started.

About This Book—And The Software That Goes With It

The book you are about to read blends theory, real-world case studies, and technical details into a text that is, at its core, actionable. There's nothing in this book that you cannot do yourself.

I distill business into its most simplified form and show you how to use world-class metrics and an overall metrics-driven approach to management to align teams, drive valuations, increase profit, create a better culture, and do it all in half of the time you're spending now.

You might find this next point interesting: unlike many solutions for business that first began with a book and then morphed into a full-fledged company or even a software solution, this book was written after the software solution was created. In other words, the concepts here have already been placed into a solution that is in the marketplace, tested, re-tested, measured, and found successful.

That solution is Catipult.AI, found at: (https://www.catipult.ai). While you're reading, keep in mind that the software we created already does everything for you, including creating a level one strategic, metrics-based plan. We also have coaches to help you, if you need help.

Business Simplified

After running many businesses and coaching even more, it became apparent that we overcomplicate the art of building a business. We can thank your local B-School for that.

What I found in my research is that there are:

• Seven (7) core drivers that run every business in the world. A driver is a way of describing an active category of business, such as leadership, employees, customers, financial partners, cash (profit) and growth. The first and most important driver of a business is you.

• Six (6) core metrics that run every company in the world, even yours. A CEO can manage just these six and run their company in half the time it usually takes and with confidence that they are building value.

- Seven (7) elements that every well-run organization has: a three-year outcome, mission, vision, value statements, accountability and, most importantly, rhythm.

That's it. It's that simple. I'll discuss each element in detail, but really spend the bulk of the time on key performance indicators (KPIs).

You'll learn:

- How KPIs can be non-punitive and how to align all projects your company does underneath a reason for doing them,

- How to write KPIs to be clear, concise and actionable,

- The formulas for the six core KPIs and how to manage to them,

- And how to scale your company quickly by taking this methodology into your entire organization (don't forget—our software does that for you).

It is my hope that this book will help transform the way you manage your business. While there are many excellent systems out there, the one that you will read about here is flexible enough to work in any situation and with any method you may be currently using.

If you're not using anything else, consider implementing *World-Class Speed*. If you are using another system, then consider using these concepts to add jet fuel to what you're already doing.

In the end, we all want more time back to focus on our legacy. That's what this book will do—give you time back.

CHAPTER 1:
JETS AND
WORLD-CLASS

"Flying is learning how to throw yourself to the ground and miss."

–Douglas Adams

In an article on September 12, 2023, *Fortune.com* announced that Boeing is letting top executives work in small offices near their homes.[1] They will **commute by private jet rather than relocate** to Boeing's new headquarters.

So, besides the obvious fact that they can build their own private jets and therefore can use their own tools to serve their leaders' needs, what does Boeing know that you don't?

They understand speed. They know that it can be a positive disruptor in business. By offering speedy transportation to their executives, the decision makers at Boeing also provided their top employees with a major benefit. More important than disrupting their business in a positive way by offering their executives a luxury commuting experience, they've also given executives a gift, because while they have built a new corporate headquarters, ***they have not done so at the expense of disrupting the personal lives of their executives.***

What Is A Private Jet, Really?

A time-saving device, sure. It represents a fantastic form of efficiency.

A money-making device, too, if you think like Grant Cardone, always on the lookout for ways to increase your business tenfold. A way to spend eight million dollars to make two hundred million. Success breeds success.

A symbol of "sitting in the back" where the real deals are made, too, rather than sitting up front where you must stress over piloting the bird.

But beyond all that, it's also a symbol of success and freedom for many hard-working entrepreneurs. While speaking at a Vistage group, I listened in on a discussion about using NetJets® and/or owning a private jet. Several of those Vistage group members had flown in a private jet somewhere at one time and they were all talking about it. "One day," someone said, "I'm going to get that subscription to NetJets or have the company buy a plane."

Like I mentioned in the introduction, the jet is a symbol of success and also the least important success factor of this group and any others. It ranks dead last in most entrepreneurs' list of things to have, well behind leaving a legacy, giving to charity and being decent parents, friends and community leaders.

The Keys To Success

We'll continue to explore the jet a bit more, as its mechanics hold the keys to success for every business. A jet is a risky machine in theory. Think about it. You enter a tin can with two engines that burn oxygen and jet fuel strapped to it and fly at altitudes over 20,000 feet through the air.

The only way such a contraption became desirable is because its very design has efficiency, accountability, transparency, and clear metrics built into its mechanics. Jets have redundant systems that talk to each other to guarantee accuracy. Success metrics are clearly defined and transparent to the pilots. Only the metrics that matter to safe flight are measured and reported.

When you step into that jet, you're stepping into a world-class machine and a world-class operation. Anything less, and you're in trouble.

World-Class Isn't Just For The Big Companies

Your business is no different. Yet, many owners believe operating as world-class is something only the big companies can do. 100 percent of the business owners I've surveyed will pick a *Fortune* 100 company as an example of a world-class operation. None have picked their own company or even a smaller business in their orbit. That's a sad statistic, considering most employees in the United States and the global economy work for small business owners.

It's also sad given the tremendous benefits of operating as a world-class company.

What Is World-Class?

Well, that's the problem. 100 percent of the owners I've worked with and/or spoken with didn't have a clear definition of world-class, either. I can't blame them. It's an overused set of words that may have always had an ambiguous, subjective definition, which by its very nature, would be impossible to achieve.

Some think world-class is operating to industry standards. Others felt it was operating above standards. Others thought it had to do with customer service or employee engagement. Answers were all over the map.

World-class simply means operating on world-class <u>structure</u> and world-class <u>metrics</u> that are guaranteed to get you the benefits listed on the following page.

3

World-Class Structure (+) World-Class Metrics = World-Class Company

The by-products of operating as world-class are that you will likely be above average in comparison to your industry, across the board.

- Higher than average quality output.

- Better than average efficiency.

- Lower than average waste of both materials and time.

- Better than average workplace safety numbers.

- Better than average on-time delivery.

- Better than average pay and benefits.

- Better than average margins.

- Better than average growth.

- Better than average culture.

Being World-Class doesn't mean being perfect. Even world-class businesses have room for improvement; in fact, the minute you think you don't have room for improvement, you're probably at risk of NOT being World-Class.

World-Class Foundation

For over 100 years, the Rockefeller Habits[2] have been the standard for world-class structure. Created by John D. Rockefeller– who owned just about everything at one point and built a great skating rink in Manhattan– these ten simple habits form a structure that most, if not all *Fortune* 500 companies operate upon. There's practically no way to get into that cohort without having this structure in place.

Let's look at each habit. As you do, quietly evaluate your company. Does your company operate this way? Never, sometimes, or habitually.

1. Healthy and aligned executive team

What does healthy mean? Yes, we're talking about physical, mental, emotional, and spiritual health. Think about the last time you had to deal with someone on your executive team who wasn't healthy: experiencing alcohol

4

addiction, grieving the loss of a spouse (by death or divorce), or experiencing some kind of existential angst, all of these can throw off the balance. A private jet with an aileron (wing flap) that's stuck will soon be in a tailspin.

2. Everyone is in alignment around the number one most important thing

What is the most important thing in your company? Does everyone else know what that thing is? Is it safety, like an aircraft manufacturer? Is it security, like a bank? Accuracy (accounting)? Purity (bottled water)? Empathy with customers? What is everyone making sure to prioritize every day?

3. Rhythmic and structured meetings

Meetings are valued when they are held regularly, kept concise, involve only those who need to attend, begin with a prioritized agenda, stay on track, and make sure to stop rabbit trails immediately. People who have nothing to contribute are allowed to leave.

4. Clear accountability for everyone

Every person in the company knows what is expected of them and who they report to for those expectations, when and how often.

5. Consistent and repeatable employee feedback

Anonymous surveys or 360° reviews are conducted with regularity; the CEO can see employee metrics on a regular basis.

6. Consistent and repeatable customer feedback

See #5 above.

7. Values and purpose are aligned within the business

It's bad enough if the owner says honesty and integrity are core values but everyone knows he's cheating on his taxes. On the positive side, when a company owner says she values funding orphanages and everyone participates in a monthly celebration of funding an organization in Haiti providing food and clean water for orphans, the values and purpose are aligned, as what's done

5

with a percentage of the profit is in alignment with stated values.

Alignment motivates an executive team and can even provide a healthy pride in craftsmanship for each individual punching aluminum sheets in a machine or crunching numbers in a spreadsheet.

8. Every employee is able to articulate the strategy

Tactics are the only thing you want to give to soldiers who might be taken as prisoners of war while charging up a mountain. But in any business situation where transparency doesn't come with risk, letting everyone know the big picture is helpful: you may have future CEOs and other big picture thinkers running things on the floor; if they don't know the strategy, they can get bored and become a competitor (and they might do that anyway, so the risk is worth the investment).

9. Every employee knows how to have a great day or week: quantitatively

Whether you have people working on piece rate, billing client hours, or making sales calls, there's nothing in a business that can't be tracked so that on Friday afternoon, when it's time to punch out, people know if they're getting the job done or not.

10. The plans and performance expectations are visible to everyone in the organization

Not only does each person know what the strategy is and what their own expectations are, they also know what's expected of their team members, their own managers, and even the executive team above their managers. Again, this requires vulnerability. Are you and your team willing to be accountable to the workforce?

Summary

If you're not entirely operating on these ten habits, don't feel bad. Most companies are not, which is good news for you. Bad news for the economy, but good news for you. These habits are your competitive advantage. They also give you more time back.

The one drawback is that they can be tough to implement with limited resources. One coaching company told my clients that they would help implement all ten habits over two years. Two years! That's far too inefficient for today's speed of business. It was great for the consultant who wanted to rack up some amazing fees, but needlessly slowed the company down.

When I saw proposals like this, I thought they were less like a jet and more like a moped.

Fortunately, you're going to learn how to implement all ten Rockefeller habits at once, in just minutes, with the resources you currently have.

World-Class Metrics

Structure without metrics is dangerous. While many companies find success and efficiencies for the first year, they also may be gaining efficiencies for the wrong strategy. Running faster in the wrong direction isn't a desired outcome.

Fortunately, world-class metrics tell us what needs to be built for us to achieve our desired outcome. These metrics are known and proven and when working toward them in the structure provided by the Rockefeller Habits, you'll gain incredible efficiencies and reduce your stress load.

In fact, there are six metrics that run every company in the world regardless of size or industry. We'll talk about those later. Before we get there, take a moment to imagine what your life as an owner would be if you only really had to manage six metrics.

One of my clients asked their CFO to produce a list of metrics to focus on. The CFO came back a week later with a list of 1,240 metrics. Another CFO at a different company produced 46 dashboards for their CEO. Both came to me in the same group meeting and initiated a WTF conversation with the rest of the group. Our meeting was derailed because every other owner had the same problem and didn't know which metrics needed their focus.

Focus

One of the hardest things for owners to do is focus. In fact, business owners, as a class, have the highest percentage of ADHD (present company included). The last thing we need is a spreadsheet of 1,240 metrics.

Implementing a world-class structure with core world-class metrics as guidance immediately creates focus and focus creates speed. The only way a jet flies safely from one point to another is if the pilots can focus on the right metrics. Sure, there may be 5,280 things happening simultaneously on the plane, but distracting the pilots with all of them would increase the chances of error.

World-class metrics need to be few and focused at the top and cascade down quickly and systematically into the rest of the organization through supporting KPIs.

You'll see how to do that later in this book.

CHAPTER 2:
THE COMPONENTS
OF A WORLD-
CLASS COMPANY
AND PROCESS

Several years ago, I began to research the components of world-class companies. I wondered what makes them move, adjust, and scale. Unfortunately, there was not one single source that clearly defined what a world-class company was. Some sources existed that defined world-class for various industries and others defined world-class by the characteristics such organizations exhibited. Among those characteristics were stamina, agility, and competitiveness. Still others discussed excellent cash management, employee management, customer relations and maintaining a solid understanding of customer needs.

It occurred to me that most of what I read focused on the outward results that a world-class company delivers. They defined standards by looking at the outside, not really what was inside the company generating those results.

We can all look at companies like Apple®, Google®, Tesla®, Coca-Cola® and many others and assume they must clearly be world-class by what we see. That exercise, however, has little relevance to SMB companies whose owners often conclude that world-class is for "the big guys."

While that may appear to be a solid conclusion, it's not a true statement. Behind the results we observe, which define in our minds what it means to be "world-class," are seven components that all companies of any size can— and should—have as their operational foundation. These components are so simple that they can be deployed immediately, even when a company is just starting. These seven components generate the outward results we define as world-class. Any company that uses them will, as a result, become a world-class organization that is visible as such to their employees, customers, investors, competitors, and industry. We'll talk about the benefits of operating as world-class in a moment. First, let's look at these seven components.

THE SEVEN COMPONENTS
of world-class companies®

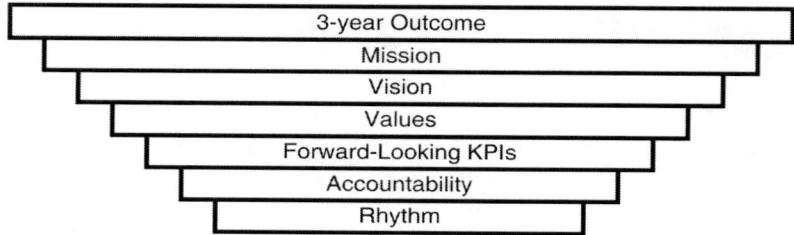

The Seven Components Of A World-Class Company

Per the graphic, every company that's considered world-class functions via these core seven components, based on the definition and guidance provided in the Rockefeller Habits. They all have three-year outcomes (in addition to shorter and longer-term objectives), clear mission, vision, and value statements (we'll cover these later), forward-looking KPIs, an accountability system, and an operational rhythm.

It's this last component, rhythm, that keeps it all running. Without it, the rest are just bits and bytes stored on a hard drive somewhere. It's also the component that trips up most SMB companies.

The good news here is that this list is only seven items long. From it will stem an entire, fast-paced process that drives incredible results.

Before we get into the process, let's break business down to simple, scalable terminology.

The Seven Business Drivers

While sitting at a dinner with several business owners, I became aware of the language we were using to talk about our businesses. As we described various challenges and successes, the nouns we were using were very basic. We talked about problems with *cash*, hiring the right *employees*, finding a great *leadership* team, managing *customer* expectations, dealing with our *financial partners*, and overall business *growth.* As the conversation ebbed and flowed, we also touched upon some personal things like where people were headed for vacation and even regrets about missing important life events.

As we talked, we discussed things we needed to do or not do within those various contexts. In other words, we were naturally discussing our businesses in common language, not in business-school jargon, as we described what we wanted and needed our teams to do in those categories.

Unfortunately, that easy-to-understand context ended at dinner. The next morning, as we all went back to work, we were managing our business within a different context: business silos. Sales, Marketing, Operations, Finance, Customer Service, and HR were the contexts we had back at the office.

The challenge with business-language silos for business owners is that we quickly lose insight into the overall goals and what each department is doing to forward a single goal. Instead, each department has its own goals filled with jargon. Meanwhile, owners have spent too much time and energy playing the band leader and hoping everyone will play a decent tune.

Weeks later, I sat down to write a presentation for the Vistage® peer board of CEOs that I was running. It was a Saturday morning when the concept became clear: using common vernacular to describe business operations is not only an easier platform for strategic thinking, but it also makes it easier to align all departments under a common goal (KPI). It would be much easier to manage a company this way. Rather than reviewing each silo, I envisioned a system where any owner could click on a corporate KPI and see the major action items each department (head) was doing to achieve it.

This structure creates scalability. Employees at any level don't need to have *cash*, *growth*, and the other basic terms defined for them. Everyone already knows what those words mean. Culture could change quickly when employees could directly associate what they were doing with a reason for doing it and the business driver it impacted. Even people who aren't big-picture thinkers love to know how what they're doing at any moment fits into a master plan.

"Today I'm helping increase cash in the business by reducing expenses associated with subscriptions we no longer need," seems much more exciting than, "My boss is on some kick to kill subscriptions and now I have to go department by department to see what they are using and aren't."

When owners can quickly align even mundane tasks with a higher-level purpose, business can change. The language we use is important, because clarity is important. Using clearly defined language eliminates the time-wasting frustration caused by ambiguity.

As I brainstormed through my presentation that Saturday morning, The Seven Business Drivers™ were born. They are, in this order:

1. You

2. Leadership

3. Employees

4. Customers

5.   Financial Partners

6.   Cash

7.   Growth

We're going to use this structure and context throughout the book. Before then, let's explain each driver.

Driver #1: YOU

The first and most important driver is you. If you aren't healthy, aligned and integrated, or in balance, don't expect your executive team or employees to be. Eventually, your customers and investors will suffer, and cash problems and growth challenges are sure to follow. *You* must put on your own oxygen mask first. We'll be discussing KPIs for you, personally, in the next chapter.

Driver #2: LEADERSHIP

Your health and vision fuel the second most important driver: Your executive team. If your executive team is healthy mentally, physically, and emotionally, and has taken ownership of your vision, then your company will also be more likely to excel. Owners who focus on giving their executive team the resources they need to be successful also learn the fine art of delegation and live happier lives. The only two drivers you should really focus on as an owner are the first two. The leadership team will handle the rest. (Don't confuse these two drivers with the six KPIs I'll suggest that every owner should be tracking.)

Driver #3: EMPLOYEES

Richard Branson, the famed founder and CEO of the popular Virgin brand claims his key to success is putting employees first, customers second and investors third. This strategy has given him a 98 percent retention rate. Branson, who is also known for his integration of work, life, and health, takes the time necessary to care for his own well-being so that he can put employees (which includes his management team) first. In other words, there is little difference between his strategy and the priority order of the first three business drivers we're covering.

What does it look like to focus on employees?

We'll discuss items that will help transform your culture and increase productivity, accountability, and retention, once you get them in place. We'll also discuss employees in more depth in Chapter 9: People.

Driver #4: CUSTOMERS

Culture, vision, pace, productivity, focus and creativity all start with the way the leader—and their leadership team—operates. How the business owner shows up to themselves and what they demonstrate to their executive team will be the traits that manifest among employees.

Once the owner, leadership team, and employees are in alignment on vision and culture as well as productivity and focused KPIs, you can truly begin to innovate and create ways to serve. Therefore, customers are the fourth priority of focus in a successful business. Happy customers are often repeat buyers and tend to give referrals, too.

The Internet has changed the way marketing works. Inbound leads rather than an outbound sales approach are fast becoming the number one source of new business. Inbound leads are those that come from: 1) referrals, 2) content you have published, 3) customer reviews and 4) networking. Another trend, especially as the millennial generation continues its march into maturity, is the "experience" customers have with your brand. Customers want a more intimate experience with the products they purchase—whether it is a business-to-business product or service or consumer product.

"A brand is the sum of all the emotions, thoughts, images,
history, possibilities, and gossip that exist
in the marketplace about a certain company."

— Luke Sullivan, *Hey, Whipple, Squeeze This:*
The Classic Guide to Creating Great Ads

All it takes is a few people with very negative strong emotions, or an unfortunate bit of gossip, to damage your brand. Because of how easy it is for one unhappy customer to impact the chatter in the marketplace about your company, customer experience – for everyone – is paramount. Consider the story of Canadian musician Dave Carroll, whose guitar was broken by an unrepentant airline whose customer service employees had no ownership of the brand and were both unable and unwilling to compensate Carroll for damages. The frustrated musician wrote a song and produced a comical YouTube video about his tribulations, it went viral, and when it did, the airline lost 10 percent of their value overnight.[3]

Driver #5: FINANCIAL PARTNERS

Financial partners are the bankers, investors, and creditors who help keep your company in business. They shouldn't be your focus but need to be part of your business thought process. Without financial partners in place, risk increases exponentially. Two of the KPIs I coach owners to have as focuses in this category are six months of operational cash available in a line of credit and 100 percent of the credit paid off quarterly.

Driver #6: CASH

I realize that placing cash as the sixth most important of seven drivers in business may be a controversial position to take. Many systems view cash as a primary driver for the business. After all, cash, it is often said, is the life blood of a company. You've probably heard the phrase "Cash is King." And it's true: If you don't have cash or at least cash flow, it's tough to have a business at all.

Cash, however, is only a result of having the previous business drivers in place. If your company is working smoothly and in alignment and sells anything of any value, you'll have customers, and customers create cash. Profitability, collections, and cash management are all components of generating cash.

Driver #7: GROWTH

The axiom "if you aren't growing, you're dying" sums up everything I'm going to say about growth. I haven't yet coached any business owner who did not agree with this universal life principle. That said, there's a common blind spot many of my clients have demonstrated, where they were deceived into thinking that just because they are growing revenue, profits or both, that they aren't "dying." The surprising truth—you can grow and shrink in business simultaneously. For example, you could grow market share, but do so in a rapidly shrinking market, and end up like Blockbuster, not realizing that the way people consume a product (in that case, movies) is about to change forever.

A World-Class Process, Based On Speed

Now that we've covered the Rockefeller Habits, the seven components of a world-class company, and the seven business drivers, it's time to move into a process that quickly generates a world-class company.

The graphic is what we call the turbine of success. The rest of this book is going to follow the structure you see in the turbine, in the specific order of the arrows.

As we mentioned, "You" are the first driver to success. You must take care of yourself and your family first.

16

Rebecca is the CEO of a $40 million manufacturing company. She had two children that were headed to college and a 401(K) for herself. When we started to review her personal outcome statement, she told me she hoped to be able to pay for her children's undergraduate degrees and said she was behind on her retirement. I was shocked. Her business was running a solid profit, so I dug a bit deeper. She had $500,000 in her retirement account and nothing in college savings accounts. She did, however, have $4 million in cash in the business. She was stressed, to say the least.

Here's how the conversation went:

Rebecca: The personal side of my finances is adding stress to my marriage. We just don't have enough saved for college (nothing) and our retirement account is way behind where our advisor says it should be.

Peter: You have $4 million in cash in the business.

Rebecca: Yes, but I like to keep it there for rainy days to keep the business going.

Peter: How much cash on hand does your CFO say you need to operate the business without much disruption?

Rebecca: $1.5 million in reserves is his target.

Peter: So that leaves $2.5 million that could be moved?

Rebecca: I suppose so.

Peter: You need to put you first. Doing so protects the business.

Rebecca: How so?

Peter: If, when I leave your office today, I fall on the concrete and break my head, that $4 million will be mine. If, on the other hand, $2.5 million is moved into your retirement and college accounts, only $1.5 million would be at risk in a lawsuit. How would you feel with $2.5 million in your personal accounts—also knowing that you could lend it back to the business with interest at any time the business may need it?

Rebecca: Relieved. Very relieved. My marriage would probably be in better shape, too.

Peter: Your marriage will be in better shape.

Rebecca: Yes, the college issue is stressing us out. My husband is a teacher and I haven't been paying myself nearly what I should from the business because I want to keep it running.

Peter: So, you're serving the business and not the other way around.

Rebecca: I guess you could say that, yes.

Peter: What are you going to do to change that today?

Rebecca: I'm going to tell my husband about this discussion and instruct my CFO to move $2.5 million over to accounts we'll set up.

Peter: When?

Rebecca: I'll have the money moved before our next meeting.

Peter: Excellent. I'd better go crack my head on your concrete before then.

When you consider your needs, your business plan needs to be one that supports them, not the other way around...and good things can happen for both. We're going to talk about personal and business outcome statements and how incredibly powerful they are for you and your employees to have in the next chapter.

The next stop on the wheel is mission, vision, and value statements— hallmarks of world-class organizations. They need to be in line with the owner's personal and business outcome statements.

We'll then talk about the focused, world-class metrics and explore the core six that will make your life much easier and business management incredibly efficient.

To achieve the metrics, teams need to do things. We call those things action items, which are part of the "activity" layer of your business. Each action item supports a metric, and I'll show you how to eliminate all actions in your business that aren't supporting a metric.

Without rhythm, however, none of the above will have any impact on your company. World-class companies operate on a rhythm and that rhythm takes place through meetings and accountability to the metrics and action items. Rhythm gets the turbine spinning. The faster it spins, the shorter your meetings can become and the more efficient your operation will be.

As the rhythm spins the turbine, most issues that occur in the business will be associated with a metric. We'll show how this direct association helps move the company forward and increases clarity for everyone.

Finally, we'll talk about people. This section is last not because it is the least important. Quite the opposite. Companies that don't have mission, vision, and value statements, aren't guided by world-class metrics, or lack an action plan to achieve them, don't know who to hire or whether the right employees are in the right seats.

When this turbine is implemented, all ten Rockefeller Habits will be in place. We'll talk about the software solution I alluded to earlier that makes all of this happen in *minutes*. But first, let's dig into the turbine and get going.

CHAPTER 3:
START WITH YOU

"A world-class company is an organization that has innovated a product or service, and by doing so, has created a unique value for its clients in the marketplace. The company doesn't necessarily have to be first, but it must create a distinction between other companies in the industry. The importance of the 'you' driver in a world-class company is vital to ensure the leaders have a plan of execution to become the very best version of themselves to raise the bar for the continued advancement and scalability of the company."

– Derrick Christy, CEO of Approved Mortgage Corporation

It's Personal, Not Just Business

I don't know anyone who started a business just to become a W-2 employee of that business. When I started my first business, I wanted to own it and have it fund my personal goals to become a cinematographer, take surfing lessons, travel the world, and spend time with my family.

Starting With You Isn't Selfish

I'm going to say something very bold. Starting with you isn't selfish; it is necessary. If you don't put your oxygen mask on first, how can you help others? How can you drive a successful business that will scale if you don't take care of yourself first?

Starting with you is like strapping a jet turbine onto a Honda Civic. The power for change is immense and the speed at which change happens will surprise you. Other leading operating systems leave this out, and while the business owners who use those systems may find other ways to achieve their personal goals, what we are talking about here is holistic. It's totally intertwined: Your business is supporting your life, because you know what you want from life, and what you want to give to others with your life.

In general, how many business owners do you know who started with themselves? In my experience, the answer is: very few. The ones who do, however, have a different perspective on their own life, and therefore, on their business, too. I remember meeting a few of these at an event called the Power Room. As I networked there, I noticed that while many of the people I was meeting were incredibly hard workers, they also had a clear sense of what they would do for their business and what they needed to delegate.

Many of them also weren't focused on building just one business, but rather a dynasty of businesses. They were always looking for ways to have other people fund their lifestyle by offering a product or service in exchange for cash. Also notable was the general size of their businesses: From five to twenty million dollars. That's small, but when you own three or four businesses with that revenue, your income can be quite large.

A common thread among these owners was the core value of having a good team. It was their priority. The only way they could attend the Power Room conferences in exotic locations was because they had good teams running the organization. If you think that's selfish, think about all the employees who had jobs because these visionaries were able to lead people while others managed processes.

The world needs visionary leaders who understand that taking care of their health, their families, and their souls are the most essential thing they must do before they can take good care of their businesses. If you're a visionary leader, the world needs people like you, because without these kinds of people there are no companies: no construction or manufacturing, no shipping and logistics, no retail, no business services.

Curt Experiences The Power Of Starting With Himself

I had the privilege to work with Curt, the CEO of Endangered Species Chocolate, a category leader in the organic chocolate industry. His brand is sold globally in Whole Foods®, Kroger®, and many others stores. (His story is shared with permission, as are all other examples where people and their companies are specifically named.)

When I first sat down with Curt and asked him what his personal three-year outcomes were, Curt initially said that wasn't important. He'd hired me to coach his business, not as a "life coach." But I asked him to humor me. Soon I learned that Curt had two dreams: (1) to take the month of July off without interruption; and (2) for his company—which gives 10 percent of its net profits back to charities that protect endangered species—to give three times more money away in a single year than the company gave the previous year. Curt viewed these two goals as both hard to achieve and completely disassociated from each other.

I believe that there are millions of people around the world just like Curt. They have a passion for doing something, but the requirements of their business or job combine with financial and other pressures to create a negative tamping force on the aspirations and life goals that are trying to surface, stuffing them underground.

These opposing forces create tremendous tension that can manifest outwardly in anxiety, depression, irritability, apathy, resignation, and even physical conditions like heart disease. Not surprisingly, heart disease is the number one killer in the United States, the world's capital of capitalism, according to the Centers for Disease Control and Prevention's website.

The Western Pendulum

This tension is caused in part by what I call the Western Pendulum. The term 'Western' is widely used to distinguish between capitalistic societies and their non-capitalistic counterparts around the world. While the term's etymology points to the geographic origination of modern capitalism in the United States, the term Western in this context no longer has geographic boundaries. It's merely used as an association with the work ethic and ideals that influence capitalistic cultures around the world.

In these societies, work is considered the pivotal point of life. Non-work-related activities—what we call our "personal life"—take second priority to the work we feel we must do to provide an income to support a "nice life."

Many business owners and entrepreneurs stepped out on their own because of their desire to balance and control their personal side of living. Perhaps they saw their own boss jetting off to the Bahamas and said to themselves, why couldn't that be me? I'm smart, and more to the point, I have ideas that could change the way this or that is done for the better. But after just a short time, they found themselves on the wrong end of the pendulum, controlled by the very business that was supposed to give them more time and freedom to chase their passions. In some cases, where business is the passion, the same thing still occurs.

Our personal life is swung back and forth, minute after minute, day after day, month after month, and year after year in a seemingly directionless, random sway that almost insures us against achieving our dreams. One minute we're scheduled to be at our child's soccer game, or school play, and the next minute we're called back into the office for an "emergency" that takes us away from the life events we said that we considered most important. Vacations are planned and then canceled. Even savings are drained to cover the salaries of employees we don't want to lose during a downturn.

It starts to feel like we are working for the business rather than the business working for us; that we are working in the business and not in it. The dreams we had when we started a business— like taking vacations or spending more time with family— often melt away into nothing but an impossible mirage. As

24

business swings us back and forth, the time we have on earth continues to wane. The tail is wagging the dog.

Regaining Control

Soon, we may feel like victims held hostage by a monster we created. We aren't victims, however, and likely didn't always have that mentality. We do have power, choices, and a free will capable of changing our trajectory. If we didn't know how to exercise that free will at one point in our lives, we probably would have found some status quo job. But that's good news: it means we can exercise that free will again!

It's important to realize that one of the reasons our minds begin to frame the business activities we do (work) as things that must be done is rooted in the survival instinct that drives us to earn money to buy food, shelter, and other items we need to live. Activities that don't immediately seem to impact survival are held in tension and incongruence with those that do. When this happens, our mind is creating an imbalance that may generate anxieties, frustrations, and a false sense of victimhood.

The truth is, there is nothing you absolutely must do, and you can become a victim of your perception in the way your situation occurs.

Don't judge yourself, though, if this has been your situation for some time. Most, if not all, humans embody this stress and viewpoint of their world and their power (or lack thereof) to change it.

Proven Concepts

The concepts presented here, including the twelve-quarter process, are proven to work, are simple to execute, and do not add to your workload; in fact, they are geared to relieve your workload and empower your executive team, and the people they lead as well. While the process is simple, the initial concept of fusing personal life and business may initially occur as counterintuitive to achieving success in either of those areas.

The integration of life and work (instead of this impossible tightrope walk attempt at balancing life and work) is a decidedly non-Western idea, but without it...you cannot be World-Class.

Here's how our conversation went:

Curt, like many CEOs, struggled at first to see how balance can grow the business.

> Peter: What do you want in twelve quarters?
>
> Curt: In my business?
>
> Peter: In your life; they are the same. What is it you want?
>
> Curt: I've always wanted to take the month of July off with my family. But I can't do that.
>
> Peter: Okay. Let's open your outcome statement with that: "The year is 2019, and I am spending the month of July with my family without interruption from the business."
>
> Curt: I still don't see what vacation has to do with my business plan.
>
> Peter: What's stopping you from taking four weeks off now?

At this point, Curt paused and looked around the room at his peer board members and then back at me.

> Curt: Okay. I think I get it. I can't take them now because I haven't developed my executive team to the level where I can leave the company for four weeks and know it will be fine. I've run a CEO-centric business.
>
> Peter: The year is 2019, and I'm taking the month of July off, uninterrupted, with my family. How are you going to make that happen?
>
> Curt: I need to spend the next twelve quarters developing my management team.
>
> Peter: What else might happen when your management team is stronger?
>
> Curt: Perhaps my revenue and profits would increase at a faster pace.
>
> Peter: The year is 2019, and I'm taking the month of July off, uninterrupted, with my family and my company's donations to fulfill its brand promise have increased 300 percent over 2016 levels.
>
> Curt: I'll write it down.

After identifying it as the goal, he then realized that the reason he couldn't take time off now and hadn't been able to do so for eighteen years is that he had been managing the company as what he called 'a CEO-centric organization.'

We dipped our toes in the CEO-centric organization at the very beginning of the book. Remember how Grant Cardone suggested that the good stuff happens in the back of the private jet? The CEO who sits in the pilot's seat is running a CEO-centric organization.

Curt's leaders were far too dependent on him. To take the vacation, he needed a different management structure in place before July 2019. He began building two tiers of management with directors and managers. He started efforts to reshape the company culture to become more empowered to make decisions without him and allow his team to be less fearful of failing. He brought in consultants to train the company in the Rockefeller Habits.

His movement and action to create a world in which he could take four weeks off from the business began by ignoring the limiting belief that the business couldn't live without him. This led to a choice he made to create a world in which he could be absent from the business for four contiguous weeks, which then created a plan and actions that were filtered throughout the entire company. The result of simply bending the business around a personal goal to take more vacation time dramatically reshaped his organization and made it stronger and more valuable.

Curt didn't stop with vacation time. He chose to have Endangered Species Chocolate give $1 million—10 percent of its net profits—away to charities that protect endangered species around the world. To do that by his deadline, he'd have to double profits. A stronger management team free to make more decisions is one way to help get profits up over three years. If profits are up, revenues likely are as well. (I know his plan did not call for cost-cutting his way toward increased net profit.)

"Before I engaged with this twelve-quarter process," Curt said, "I would say 'someday' I'll do this or that. Now, I am dissecting everything that needs to happen for my 'someday' to be realized and then executing those things within twelve quarters. I believe the real power behind this process is that it allows one to run a company with intention. The message of having the business work for me and not the other way around actually spoke to me. It made me realize that while I valued time with family more than time on business, my life wasn't reflecting that as consistently as I would have liked. I don't want that time to slip away, and now I'm operating in a way that it won't."

Toward the end of July 2018, Curt called me and said something like this: "Peter, I've only made two work-related phone calls from the cabin this month… and this is the second one, to call you. I just wanted to let you know we've had an awesome time as a family here for the last four weeks, and I want to thank you for encouraging me to start with my own three-year outcome in mind."

"The process lets you pick who you want to become or accelerate who you already are. It's a life accelerator. Instead of feeling like you must do life, the twelve-quarter process changed the way life occurred to me and empowered me to take 100 percent control of my life—with no excuses. And then drive each day to make it happen."

—Ken Thieneman, CEO of Thieneman Construction, Inc.

18 Months Or 36 Months?

Here's even better news: while Ken and Curt refer to a three-year process, the stark reality is that most who implement the ideas I'm sharing in this book will achieve their goals in 18 months. The phenomenon became so much of a pattern that I reached out to a psychologist friend of mine to find out what was happening. He wasn't surprised. He said one of the most powerful tools psychologists and therapists use in their practice is linking actions to consequences. When business owners realize that the way they are running their business is having an adverse effect on their personal goals and life, he said, then change happens quickly as the desire to fight for lost time takes over.

To drive the point home even further, I changed the contracts my coaches use with their clients from 12 quarters to just six. We still use a three-year vision, because that's the psychological time of greatest believability, but we know that most will achieve their outcomes much sooner.

World-Class Mindset

Your mindset as a leader is everything. How you think is how you occur and what you become. One of the biggest inhibitors to growth and good management is the pervasiveness of limiting beliefs. A hallmark of world-class leaders is self-awareness, especially when it comes to their own personal belief system. It's for that reason that we're going to dive into your mind for just a few moments. As you read the rest of this chapter, keep in mind that your employees have the same things going on in their head. Exposing them to these ideas can really help grow a positive culture.

"Don't be intimidated by what you don't know.
That can be your greatest strength and
ensure that you do things differently
from everyone else."

—Sara Blakely, founder of Spanx

Introjections And Biases

There are two primary types of limiting beliefs: (1) an introjection; and (2) bias. An introjection is a term coined by Fritz Perls, the founder of Gestalt therapy. An introjection is an idea imposed upon us by society, religion, parents, peers, and our environment. Introjections become limiting beliefs that our mind can perceive as actionable truth. Bias is simply anything you currently think to be true that limits the options you perceive to exist, and consequently, the actions you take. Both introjections and biases fall under the broad umbrella category of limiting belief.

Another way to think about limiting beliefs is to picture a horse wearing blinders. These black leather squares are placed to the sides of the horse's eyes to block its peripheral vision. The horse can only see what is directly in front of it, thus reducing the possibilities for action it perceives to only those presented by the immediate situation. Blinders are perfect for horse racing because they force the horse to rely on the jockey for all strategic decisions and prevent it from being swayed by distractions.

29

You don't have a jockey, however, to guide your decisions and frame the field of play. But you do have blinders on, and they severely restrict the options you perceive to exist.

Most of us—myself included—don't think we have limiting beliefs because they are beliefs. And that's the fundamental problem. If we believe something is true, then we don't perceive it as limiting our actions but rather guiding them. We see what is in front of us and not the blinders, in other words.

Most limiting beliefs first occur with the word "should" or "could" in front of them. Here are a few examples you may have.

- You should eat all the food on your plate because people are starving.

- You should hold a steady job because it is too risky to start your own business.

- You should vacation at Disney World®.

- You should have kids.

- You should get married.

- You shouldn't get divorced.

- You should travel more.

- You should live in this suburb.

- I shouldn't fire this employee because he's been with me for a long time.

Limiting beliefs also disguise themselves as facts.

- My business will never be a $100 million enterprise.

- I am stuck in my career because I am the breadwinner.

- A kid with Asperger's syndrome from South Africa will never become the richest, most technologically innovative person in the world.

Let's spend a minute on that last bullet point. Of course, the kid I'm referring to is Elon Musk.

Musk is well known for his billions, and his net worth makes him the wealthiest man today, although he's known as a risk-taker and therefore, he might not be the world's wealthiest man when you read this. On the other hand, it's more likely that as you're reading this, he's worth more than the estimated $247.4 Billion USD he is worth at the moment I'm writing (on September 27, 2023, Forbes reports Musk is down about 0.32 percent or $801 million, just a little blip...). But since we are talking about limiting beliefs, how Musk became wealthy, how much he's worth today (which can only be estimated) or what companies he owns now is not as interesting as an examination of his beliefs. The clues are everywhere, and of course he talks about all sorts of things in the media– sometimes it's hard to tell whether he's being serious or not. But let's talk about the letter X because this might be the biggest clue of all.

Musk sold his first company, Zip2, in 1999 for $307 million, then built PayPal, originally known as X.com. After he sold PayPal in 2002, he waited 15 years, but he loved the domain name X.com so much he bought it back in 2017. Who knows what he thought he might do with it then. Perhaps he had a plan to buy Twitter then, or perhaps he had a dozen ideas. In 2020, he and pop singer Grimes named their child X Æ A-Xii. In a photograph welcoming X to the world, Musk can be seen wearing a T-shirt that says, "Occupy Mars."

To a mathematician, X represents the unknown, laden with possibilities. Musk's fascination with naming things X, from social media platforms to human children, is perhaps the biggest indication of what he believes in. As far as Musk is concerned, when it comes to his principles, he says, "I operate on the physics approach to analysis. You boil things down to the first principles or fundamental truths in a particular area and then you reason up from there." This speaks to a discipline of looking at fundamental, objective truth, not being swayed by emotion at all. Based on his use of the letter X, we could say that "it is possible" may be Musk's favorite fundamental truth.

We all have limiting beliefs. Becoming aware of them is key to being a world-class leader. If Musk let limiting beliefs rule his life, perhaps we wouldn't have electric cars, PayPal, Star Link, SpaceX, and whatever else he's going to invent. One thing is for sure, Musk is attracted to possibility and unyielding in his pursuit of ideas that will transform the future. Think about it this way: While some entrepreneurs are trying to decide whether it is cost-effective to buy a private jet, Elon Musk is trying to figure out how to fly to Mars.

The same is true for you. If you let your limiting beliefs define your actions, what will be missing from the world, your life, your friends, and your employees? Do you see the future as laden with possibility? Or do you view the unknown with suspicion and fear?

Here's a brief exercise. Take a moment to jot down answers to these questions with whatever comes to mind.

- What are your limiting beliefs? Remember, a limiting belief will not occur as limiting. It will occur as truth.

- What occurs as true about your business or job?

- What occurs as true about your time outside of your business?

- What occurs as true about yourself?

Is what is occurring true, or could there be a different truth that someone else may hold?

> *"Truth is not what you want it to be; it is what it is,*
> *and you must bend to its power or live a lie."*
>
> – Miyamoto Musashi.

Case Study: Jennifer, CEO of D3-NYC

Jennifer is a very successful executive in the capital of marketing and advertising, New York City. With more than thirty years in the industry, Jennifer has weathered many storms, beaten dozens of competitors, and thrived in an industry known to be littered with others who just could not compete in her fast-paced world. She also cut her teeth when Madison Avenue was very much a man's world and founded one of the first woman-owned agencies in New York. She's the least likely person you'd expect to be hampered by limiting beliefs.

With Jennifer's permission, I'm sharing the list of introjections and beliefs that she continues to fight.

- I should be more productive.
- I should have gotten more done this week.
- I should have watched the cash flow more.
- I should have been more decisive.
- I should stop picking at myself.
- I should have saved more money already.
- I should have seen my sister before she left.
- I am not motivated anymore.
- I am not a good friend anymore.
- I am not a good sister anymore.
- I am not trying hard enough.
- I am not a good therapy patient.
- I am not paying enough attention to my husband.
- I am not generous.
- I am not a good leader.
- I am not fun to be around.
- I am not smart enough.
- I am not focused.
- I am not a planner.
- I am not a true entrepreneur.
- I am a pest to my kid and husband (and at work).
- I am tired.
- I am a joke.
- I am a phony.
- I am not honest.
- I am worn out.
- I am burnt out.
- I am lazy.
- I am crazy.
- I am frustrated.
- I am bored.
- I am lost.
- I am going through the motions.

Everything above bombards Jennifer daily. Despite her success with a woman-owned business in a cut-throat world, her mind still bombards her with beliefs that are false.

Jennifer's assignment was to begin writing down truths that counter each one of those beliefs. Here are two of her counters that she offered to share.

I am not productive.

Yes, I am very productive. Last night, I took a client out to dinner for several hours even though I had gotten up at 4:45 a.m. yesterday, and today I got up early, met a client early this morning to discuss business, have arranged to go with her to an event tonight, and during the day, I have a couple of meetings that I added into my schedule. I've already done a short review (thirty minutes) with my junior partners and am working on my twenty minutes [of meditation], having meditated for seven minutes on the train this morning.

I'm supposed to know all the answers.

This morning, I comfortably admitted that I was stumped for a reply from a client but that I wanted to help any way I could. I am practicing asking questions and putting less pressure on myself to be the answer girl.

Both limiting beliefs were affecting her ability to be a transformational leader. Her drive to know all the answers kept her from being able to meditate for just twenty minutes every day, a key component of transformation that I'll discuss later in the book. As she tried to quiet her mind, her belief that she must know everything compelled her to break from her quiet mind to pick up her phone and check the latest industry trade rags.

The idea that she isn't productive hampered her ability to spend time thinking strategically, as productivity was defined by getting things done. Strategic thinking isn't a task-driven exercise and doing it usually doesn't result in the immediate gratification of checking boxes off a list.

When she—or any of us—believe we aren't something, we will act under that stress in a subconscious attempt to disprove ourselves. We'll never win.

We need to change the stories we tell ourselves. And that starts by not allowing our minds to cram false ideas about ourselves into our thought streams. It will take discipline to do this and, of course, mindfulness, which is necessary to make the right choices.

Choice—The Power Behind The Universe

According to scientific theory, the universe began as a stupendous array of light and energy that exploded 13.7 billion (or so) years ago. Science isn't sure what caused the explosion of nothing into something, but many theologies point to a supernatural intelligence that chose to create a universe different from the one it originally occupied (and may still occupy, depending on your belief system) and then took the action of the big bang to bring about its will.

You too have the power to choose to take responsibility for your life and, as the Creator did years ago, create your alternate universe. An alternate universe is anything that's different from the life you are currently living. If you don't like what you are doing now or where you are living, you have the choice to change to a different occupation or place of residence. Your limiting beliefs may tell you otherwise, however, and attempt to turn you into a victim, but the truth is that choice is the ultimate power you have.

As a business owner, you may love the business you started and hate the life the business is forcing you to live. Or you could love both and have a burning desire to start something different—to give back in some way. That desire is going to weigh on you—until you make a choice.

If your desire is to maintain your status quo and do nothing differently, choosing not to change is, in fact, a choice to preserve. Those who take that path are choosing to act to maintain their current status quo. And that's okay if you love where you are. Choosing to keep the current situation requires the same intention as wanting to change it. I've coached people who love their lives but still decided to use the tools presented in this book to intentionally preserve the life they lived from distractions and opportunities that often arise.

Limiting Beliefs Become Stories

The irony of human development is that the brain frames events and experiences early in our childhood when we don't have the capacity to adequately understand what we are framing. A mental frame is a construct by which and through which we view the world.

For example, if a parent routinely tells their child that they will never succeed in life, then the child's mind may create a frame of themselves as a failure. Once firmly established by repeated comments (introjections) and experience failing to meet the parents' expectations, that mental frame may become a limiting belief that generates a life-long story: "I am a failure, and therefore, anything I try will fail."

Once believed as truth, future opportunities the child may encounter as an adult might be viewed and evaluated based on the story that failure is a likely outcome of trying. The resulting action may be to simply not plan in the first place. The same could be true of positive reinforcement during childhood. Tell a child they're a prince or princess early on and some children will believe it—and may act like a spoiled brat for the rest of their life.

The mental frame, formed by limiting beliefs, creates stories about us and our world. These stories are powerful and incredibly dangerous tools used routinely by our minds. In fact, as we learned earlier in the previous chapter, our minds tap the well of these stories and beliefs to fill in missing information and generate our truth to what we see and experience.

Here's another example:

Let's say you've had numerous experiences with employees who would sneak out of your building to use illegal drugs. After several years of this experience, your mind puts meaning to the event of employees leaving your building during work hours. It occurs to you that they are leaving to do drugs.

36

The event of an employee leaving the building during work hours means nothing. Patterns of similar events in the past associated with former employees aren't attributable to other employees in the present. If you act against a new employee who just happened to behave in a manner consistent with your mind's frame for the story that "drug abuse" is occurring, you may be compelled to take actions against the employee that aren't justified.

Stories, in other words, are dangerous. They may not be true, and they may be stopping you from building the life and business you truly desire to have in twelve quarters.

Up next are three of the top stories I've coached people through. While you're reading them, think of your own stories.

Story 1: I Don't Have Time To Focus On My Personal Ambitions

Truth: No one owns time or has it. We do, however, spend time. Time is attached to the physical world. It is the universal force of measurement that gradually drives all substances into a different form of existence. Time is running you into the ground.

We never know when we will expire, but expire, we will. That's a fact. The story in your head that you don't have time for your personal ambitions is only true if you continue to operate as if that is truth. Doing so results in inaction that only reinforces the story.

Anyone can wake up ten minutes earlier each day or go to sleep ten minutes later. Time can be spent differently if the choice is made to do so.

Story 2: I Don't Have The Resources To Execute My Vision

Truth: For those of us who live on planet Earth, this story is just an excuse. Earth has all the resources we need to accomplish any ambition. Finding them, however, takes work and time. Convincing the caretakers of those resources to let us use them also takes time (and thick skin that can stand rejection).

The truth, however, is that you do have access to the resources you need to follow your ambition. You just need to find them.

What are some of the stories in your head? Take a moment and list them on a sheet of paper. Consider:

- What stories am I telling myself about my business that are just excuses?

- What stories am I telling myself about my finances?

- What stories am I telling myself about taking time off?

Story 3: The Business Can't Live Without Me

If you feel the business can't live without you, then it may be controlling you. Most of the people I coach have a dream of "one day" spending more time with the family or taking more vacations. When I ask them what prevents them from doing so now, their consistent replies are:

- The business won't let me.

- My business is just keeping me too busy.

- If I left for two weeks in a row, my business would collapse.

- I'm in growth mode—it's all hands-on deck here.

- I'm losing revenue and shrinking now; I need to focus on getting things back in order.

While those replies may be true contemporaneously with the question being asked, they do not necessarily have to be true in the future. Well-run and managed enterprises, no matter how large or small, can—and should—be able to run without the CEO and owner on premise all the time.

Change your mantra and then begin to build the future in which the business can live without you. As you'll learn in future chapters, businesses who aren't dependent on their owner have greater valuations and more options. Leaders aren't followers and architects don't build—they control and define the shape and destiny of what others are able to help make.

Transform Your View Of Events

One of my favorite business books is *The Three Laws of Performance* by Steve Zaffron and Dave Logan[4]. I teach the laws in this book regularly to my clients. The book covers three laws that are immutable in business and life because they are true to the way human beings experience events. The first law of performance: How people perform correlates to how situations occur to them.

The word "occur" here is telling. Notice the authors didn't say "the way situations are." The reason for this important word choice is attached to what we covered previously about stories, limiting beliefs, and framings. We don't know how the situation is. All we must go by is how it occurs to us as framed by the stories, biases, and introjections in our mind. How situations occur to us is likely different than how they occur to others. Since situations occur based on biases and stories that, if we are mindful, we can identify as not true, then it is possible to change the way a situation occurs to us and then also change the actions we would take, thus, opening us up to a world of previously shuttered possibilities.

Remember the Western Pendulum? It exists primarily because our lives occur as bifurcated between personal and business. When it occurs as two separate lives, we act as if they are separate, and the result we achieve is the imbalance of working for the business rather than it is working for us.

> "My philosophy of life is that if we make up our mind what we are going to make of our lives, then work hard toward that goal, we never lose—somehow, we always win out."
>
> —Ronald Reagan

Transformation 1: There Is No Distinction Between Business Life And Personal Life

Understanding that there is no distinction between self and business is something that confounds the wisest master of business.

It confounded me, too, when I was building my companies. In fact, I never gave it much thought. The business had needs, and my "self" had needs. The two were distinguished in my mind, and therefore, manifested as completely disconnected from each other in my visible life.

Because business and life occurred that way, I had certain self-limiting beliefs that were more than just ideas. Here are just a few of the ones I had in my mind:

- Don't bring your personal issues into work.

- Business comes first because it provides the income needed to sustain you.

- The hardest workers are connected 24-7.

- To be successful as an entrepreneur, you must give your all to your business.

- If you're not on all the time, someone else will be.

- Sacrifice for the business, and you'll get a huge payout that will allow you to take time off and enjoy life with yourself and your family.

The last one on the list ruled my life. As a "start-up" guy living in the geographically compact Silicon Valley, I was surrounded by entrepreneurs who burned themselves out for one, two, or three years and had reaped the huge payout. They occurred to me as living proof that sacrificing your life for the big check was a smart move.

My ego gravitated toward this belief. I had friends who hit it big and chose to take a year off to travel the world. One of them sold his company, bought a boat, and sailed the world for a year.

It is easy to get caught up in the idea that money can be easily created with hard work and that working for money is worth what occurs as a "short-term" sacrifice.

However, any belief that separates your personal life from your business life creates a false dichotomy.

There is no separation between the two. None. All that exists is your life as framed by the time you have on the planet. The only time you are guaranteed is the present moment. The past doesn't exist. If it did, you could go back to it. The future also doesn't exist. Both are concepts formed by your mind.

The only time you are guaranteed is the present moment.

Think about it. There's just you and the present moment in which you exist. Now, let's extend that concept into the reality of business.

Stories In Your Mind About Business

Archeologists believe our human ancestors spent most of their time foraging for food and sleeping. As our species evolved, we began to make tools to help us harvest or kill food, build shelters, and craft utensils for cooking.

For most of human history, up to the Age of Industry, people lived an agrarian life focused on staying alive. Even those early entrepreneurs who ventured to create livings by providing goods or services often still had small farms or gardens and hunted for their protein.

The focus for most of our human history was on sustaining life. Activities were not separated between "work" and "personal life." It was just life and living day-to-day, moment by moment. Families lived together and supported each other in the daily grind to stay alive. The family unit was, in a way, the first business. It was real and tangible. Business was simply the activities people did.

Story 1: My Business Is Separate From Myself

In 1602, however, the activities people did to sustain life were assigned for the first time to an abstraction of reality called the East India Company. The Dutch government granted the world's first corporation exclusive rights to all trade with India, personifying the corporation as an entity bigger and with greater longevity than the investors who created it. The East India Company would continue to trade with India long after the people who originally comprised it were dead.

Since then, corporations have gradually embedded themselves into the human psyche as something almost human. Because a corporation is assigned rights and can accept liability for the actions of the people who work for it, our language now makes little distinction between the notion of a business entity that exists only on paper and a human who exists.

Consider the colloquialisms:
- I work for Company X.
- Company X is corrupt.
- Company X is growing rapidly.
- Company X is dying.
- I hate Company X.
- I love Company X.
- Company X has an outstanding mission.
- Company X has a great vision for future products.
- Company X is moving me to another state.
- My company is taking up a lot of my time.
- I need to spend time with the company.

You are also living within this tragic cultural disambiguation. Legally, there is a distinction between the business and you. The former exists for the protection of the latter. However, when this disambiguation is extended into the strategies generated for a living, and we believe that the business is separate from ourselves, then we begin to manage in two different buckets.

Story 2: I Have Two Buckets Of Time To Manage

When we believe that time is bifurcated, our mind creates one bucket of time for activities that occur to sustain life and one for everything that does not happen as life supporting. Naturally, it prioritizes the former ahead of the latter. By categorizing activities that sustain life as related to a personified concept of business only, our tendency will always be to take the currency from the personal bucket and give it to the business bucket.

Story 3: Business Alone Is The Only Life-Sustaining Activity

When we believe that our work is the only life-sustaining activity, then we prioritize our time spent into that bucket and the expense of other activities that sustain our spirit and enhance the quality of our time on earth into another bucket?

Spirit and body need to be in balance with each other. When we invest too much time in the business, we decrease the time we spend with family, our God, ourselves in meditation, community to give back, and other activities that, although not money generating, have been scientifically proven to keep our physical bodies healthy and even lengthen life.

When we serve the business at the expense of the spirit, anxiety, and depression increase—both of which take a toll on the body and can lead to its ultimate demise.

Control is an illusion. And it is an illusion that starts at home—with the self. If you are truly in control of self, then the business can't control you. In most cases, however, we look outside self at what we occur to control—cash flow, some employee behavior (more influencing and directing than controlling), product development, marketing spends and not much else.

We see ourselves as masters of our fate, leading a symphony of our making. Our egos have shackled us to our business and jobs. We believe we are invaluable and without our contribution, the business could not flourish. These ego-driven, self-limiting beliefs can stifle company growth and even lead to a company's demise.

When we choose to believe that others could run the business as well, if not better, than we are, then we are open to testing that assumption by gradually releasing control to others.

When we release control, we become more valuable to those to whom control is released and free our minds to think strategically. That freedom may release new products and services into the market and help increase the stability and long-term viability of your company and your legacy.

We only become as important as we think we are when we choose to view ourselves as expendable.

Story 4: Business Is "Someone"

Business, however, is not sentient. It is a concept that exists only in legal documents and not in reality. You cannot find or interact with Apple, Google, or any other entity that is incorporated because they don't exist.

That said, what is business or work or career? They are nothing more than words for categories of activities we do to earn a living and sustain part, not all, of our needs.

Business doesn't exist. Business-related activities, however, do exist.

- The business, while legally distinct, is not different from you. You conduct activities, some of which are related to business.

- There is only one bucket of time, not two—the time you are given.

- Your body and spirit are equally important; focusing on the survival of the body through business activities alone can lead to depression, anxiety, regret, guilt, and other negative and debilitating emotions.

- Others in the world can conduct your business activities as well, if not better, than you can.

44

To help model these changes in perspective for the rest of this book, I am going to shift from using the term business to something more accurate: business activities.

This subtle shift in language changes the way business occurs as a personified "something or someone" we serve to the reality of what it is: activities we do to earn a living. It accomplishes this shift in the following steps:

1. Without personification, it is harder to assign responsibility for your choices to something that doesn't exist. The business can't be blamed for taking too much time, for instance.

2. By not blaming others—even a personified nonentity—we accept responsibility for our choices.

3. By taking responsibility, we gain control.

4. When we gain control, what we are controlling is our time.

5. When we realize we are controlling time, we are controlling the activities we choose to do during the time we have.

6. From this new perch of personal control over our operations and responsibility for directing them, we can begin to balance our life-sustaining activities around things we want to do, not just business activities.

7. When we start to balance our time between categories of life-sustaining activities, we can then start to bend the business activities to support the goals and objectives we currently hold in high esteem and are impossible to achieve.

8. When the business activities are bent around what we want to do—those passions—we can build a plan that creates the desired outcome in twelve quarters.

Shifting Gears

We're now going to shift gears. Hopefully, this chapter has opened your mind and given you much to reflect upon. My other book *Start with You*, goes into the subjects above in more detail. For now, just remember:

1. You have stories in your mind that aren't true.

2. Time is not bifurcated into one category or another. Time is finite currency to spend.

3. You have control to make choices.

In the next chapter, you're going to make a choice by creating an Outcome Statement. For preparation, let's reflect upon the experience we already highlighted from Curt. He had a vision to spend four weeks without a phone call with his family. For ten years, he had the limiting belief that it couldn't happen. Then, he made a choice to make it happen. In 18 months, it did happen.

Curt's Start With You KPI:

Consecutive Weeks in the Cabin with My Family; Target 4 weeks; Actual: 1 week. He was at 25 percent of his target. To cover the delta, he had to train and replace members of his management team, re-organize areas of the company, and put an accountability system in place. Those became his action items. By seeing his own targets as priorities for the business and in-line with those of the business, he was able to quickly create (within just a few minutes) action items he needed to take to hit his target.

You'll be doing the same very shortly.

Industry Expert Interviews And Case Studies:

Using Catipult For Non-Profit Organizations

Dr. Steven Kirch

Tell us about your background.

I spent nine years working at IBM in New York before I made the leap to the West Coast and continued at Intel for almost 22 years.

A few years into my time at Intel, I was offered the opportunity to take a course on the *Seven Habits of Highly Effective People*. It was transformational for me. When I realized that they were looking for instructors, I put my hand up. I became a certified facilitator, and I taught that class for a number of years at Intel. Intel required senior leaders to teach three classes a year. Through that process, I got to know some people at the Franklin Covey Company and got certified in some other things, personal organizational effectiveness, productivity, and more. I really enjoyed the teaching. Seven years ago, I left Intel, but I realized I couldn't retire! I wanted to stay involved in business.

I figured I'd hang out a shingle as a productivity coach because I've been doing it for 20-plus years. The thing that I discovered was that small business owners have absolutely no clue what their time is worth. Part of that is because they're changing hats 17 times a day. But they don't know where to focus. They don't know what to focus on. But if you don't know the starting value and you don't know the ending value, how do you calculate an ROI? People would say, "What is it worth investing in a coach to help me improve the value of something that I don't understand?" Because of that, I got an awful lot of pushback. People would say, "I don't know if this is the right time. I don't know if this is worth it. I don't know if it's a good thing to do." I saw a lot of uncertainty.

Next, I got introduced to something called LPW. Soon I had refocused my coaching around improving profitability. I could get in front of a group of small business owners and say, "I can find six figures in untapped revenue for any small business in under an hour without having to spend any additional money on marketing." That was a pretty compelling message, and that system really works. My practice quickly filled up.

But, in parallel with that, as I retired from Intel, I learned they had a program called Encore Fellowship. I learned that for the successful retiree in good standing, Intel will make a donation to a nonprofit, so the nonprofit can hire that retiree for 1000 hours. I had a good friend named Randy who had founded a nonprofit called the Gratitude

Network. I asked him, "What could I do to help the Gratitude Network? The Intel Foundation will pay for it."

And he said, "Steven, we're in leadership development. We had seven people go through our fellowship last year. Some of them had a really good experience. Some of them, not so good. Can you talk to the coaches and the fellows and figure out what worked and what didn't and create a coaching program that will make it so that everybody's successful?" So, I created what we use today as our coaching program for the Gratitude Network. I became a member of the board. I'm always trying to come up with new ideas, I'm a strategy person, I'm a developer of ideas, and I read a lot. I pulled ideas from a bunch of books, *Scaling Up!, Traction*, and *The Three Hag Way*, by Shannon Susco. I took those three books and created a hybrid system for the Gratitude Network all around the Rockefeller Habits for nonprofits. I've been doing that for a couple of years. I've taken three dozen organizations, mostly nonprofits, through the Rockefeller Habits.

You've done a lot in this field. What did you think when you saw Catipult?

I was introduced to Catipult in November or December of 2022. I jumped all over it. I had created a huge spreadsheet with the KPIs, with the rocks and milestones, (although the rocks and milestones were not necessarily connected to the KPIs at that time, which is a common mistake people make). I recognized all of the value in Catipult, in comparison to my cumbersome spreadsheets. I've shown Catipult to many people and they all see the value instantly.

I call my own hybrid system the Profit Minds growth system. It's about 1) profit growth, 2) productivity, and 3) scaling.

Tell us an anecdote or two.

So here are a few stories. I met one for-profit business owner who was meeting with his leadership team every morning for 45 minutes to an hour. Every morning! Once I started working with him, we shifted to a once-a-week meeting and initially scheduled it for two hours because he wasn't convinced we could do it in less than that. I ran the first half a dozen meetings or so. And the first meeting did take us two hours. But every meeting since then has been less than 90 minutes. Most recently, the Chief of Staff ran it. And that's sort of the transition we want. I run the first few, then the chief of staff takes over, and he or she runs a few meetings with me watching, and then they're on their own. That's the normal cadence. Soon the weekly meetings didn't even take an hour.

The meeting structure is so focused. I saw this all the time in corporate meetings for thirty years: what happens is the first topic that comes up, people dig deep and solve it. And then you come to the next topic, and you solve it. But the way Catipult structures weekly meetings, you list all the issues, and you don't talk about them. Just this morning I was talking to another owner, and I asked, "Do you have a weekly meeting?"

She said, "Yes."

I said, "How long does it take?"

She said, "It's three hours."

And I said, "I know what's happening. The problem is the first topic that comes up, you dive deep into that topic. You need to resist that. Do you have somebody on your team who is good at keeping the conversation on target? Assign them the task of being that rabbit trail detector. Keeping the conversation on track and don't let everyone dig into each issue as it comes up. Just put them on the list and then prioritize them. That's the key, is just list the issues; then prioritize; then begin to solve."

If you don't get to some of the topics, that's okay. They're less important. You make sure that they get handled. Maybe there are two or three people who need to go off and solve a particular thing. And if the number one priority really is just between two people, you can say, "You guys take that offline, but make sure you deal with it right at the end of this meeting." Your team has to really focus on listing the issues before you dig in.

I also love Catipult's CHARP system because it acknowledges that sometimes the changes that happen are outside of my control, while others are in my control, and I can distinguish between them.

Let's talk about nonprofit leaders. Should they be on Catipult, too?

Yes. It's the same reason that for-profit leaders should be on Catipult, honestly. First, that whole process of where you want to be in three years is so useful, and second, the accountability chart of who's responsible for what in the organization is critical, too. The founder can stop being responsible for everything that happens in the organization. You know, intellectually, that it's not scalable or sustainable. So it's important that as you have chosen to do good in the world, you still need the organization to serve the leader, too, and the life that they want to lead. Ask yourself: three years from now, do you want to be working more than you're working now?

Even if you're in the nonprofit space, you cannot serve your demographic constantly. You have to take a break. And the same traits of the healthy CEO that you have in the for-profit space, those are the same things that you need to be healthy as an executive director, as a leader in any organization.

Any differences you'd like to highlight?

There is one thing that's a little bit tricky in the not-for-profit space that's different. In the for-profit space, the customers are also the people who pay you. In the not-for-profit space, the customers are the people that you serve, but the donors are not necessarily the same people. So, what I recommend for nonprofit leaders to do with the Catipult system is to position their donors in the Financial Partners Driver. That means that the churn of donations, the pipeline of donations, all the stuff which you would normally put under Customers, instead, that goes under Financial Partners. It's the same KPI but under a different Driver. So that's a little nuance for not-for-profits. And that's the value of having a coach alongside who can help you customize your software to your needs, someone to help you think through where the KPIs intersect with the Drivers.

When it is all said and done: Why Catipult?

If there's one good reason why people should be getting into Catipult: It's going to give you your life back. You got into this business, whether it's a for-profit or a nonprofit, because you wanted to make a difference. It wasn't about the money. You're in it because you want to serve other people. It's too easy to wind up being a slave to that enterprise. Catipult is a platform that will allow you to figure out what you need to focus on so that the business runs itself and you get your life back.

CHAPTER 4: THE OUTCOME STATEMENT

There are four major statements that you and your company need to have in place to manage effectively and align your teams. The first is an outcome statement, which is followed by the vision statement, which portrays where the company will be far in the future. The third is a mission statement, which describes the purpose the company will operate toward forever, and the fourth is

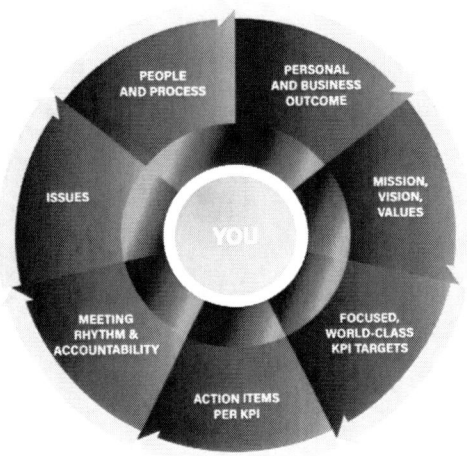

the values statement, which describes how the business will operate, culturally and behaviorally. We'll take a look at the outcome statement first. Unlike traditional outcome statements that only focus on the business, ours includes personal, professional, and business outcomes into one simple paragraph. Our outcome statement is written using a precise syntax based on psychology that is designed to help your brain not only believe in the outcome, but also continue to solve for it in the subconscious layer. It really works.

To do this, you'll draft a statement that declares how things will be in three years. We start by saying "The year is ____ and I am____." You'll fill in the first blank with the date that is three years from now.

Here's an example:

"The year is 2027. I am in great physical shape, weighing 175 pounds with 15 percent body fat. I am biking four times per week, having five dates per month with my significant other and have zero debt. Professionally, I speak at five major trade shows each year and I appear as an expert resource in top media outlets. I've read three books per quarter for 12 quarters. My business has three offices around the world with 1000 employees and a 35 percent growth rate, or 30 percent and zero corporate debt."

When you write your outcome, you'll program your brain to make it happen. Be specific: don't use words like "more" or "larger" or "great shape." Define those concepts so you can create KPIs that are measurable. If you are a member of an executive team, you should also write your outcome statement, following the exact same syntax. Make sure that your description of what the business is doing is focused on your development and complements the company's overall three-year outcome statement.

A great practice is to read your outcome statement every day. It will program your mind to make that reality happen. You'll also want to share this with your business or executive coach if you have one. Once you have the outcome, he or she can help you break this outcome statement into key performance indicators, and then milestones.

A Few Other Tips On Writing Three-Year Outcomes

Be specific. Don't say "we'll have more growth." Instead, say, "We'll have grown our top line revenue by twenty percent per year." Once you've done your personal outcomes, add a paragraph with your professional outcomes. For example, you may want to be perceived as an industry leader. "The year is 2027 and I am being invited to major industry conferences, conducting at least three keynote addresses per year." From that statement, you'll later map out a plan to make that happen.

When you repeat "The year is ____ and I am ____," if you put your personal first and your business second, it is getting past the *reticular activating system*, which is a little pea-sized thing in your brain that serves many functions including protecting you from the unknown or harm. So, when you program it with an idea that it thinks it might not be able to achieve, such as a little technique like "the year is and I am," you fool it with a declarative statement by teaching it something that has already occurred. Your brain is then going to work to solve that lesson in reverse.

Finally, your brain only solves the problems you give it. Now, from one business owner to another, I can guarantee you I give my brain way too many small problems to solve: answering emails, doing this, doing that. How are we going to meet the next quarter's objectives? Those are smaller problems. What we're really talking about is giving the brain that three-year vision as a completed possibility.

When you know it and your team knows it, then all these brains are going to start solving for that and amazing things will happen, such as picking up conversations in a bar or wherever you socialize which relate to that outcome statement, because it's permeating your brain, and your subconscious will work on it and pay attention to additional stimulation about it.

I want you to enjoy writing your outcome statement: think big, think bold, think specific, because that's the crux of it. If you want to use software to capture it, Catipult will automate measurable KPIs and action items so you can start executing it. You're going to enjoy this vision, this dream, because this is the one *You* are creating, and that's how world-class companies operate.

No, This Isn't Life Coaching

I had a CEO tell me once that he didn't sign up for this "shit." He wanted business advice. The main problem with just getting business advice and focusing on the pragmatic functions of turning a profit is that we are…well, human. Our problems in business are always tied to internal issues that have nothing to do with our business. That's about all the 'therapy' I'll get into today, but for anything else I have to say in this book to work, you need to play along with the Outcome Statement. It is quite possibly the most powerful tool you'll have to achieve your objectives quickly. On top of that, giving this gift to your employees is priceless. It's also like adding hydrogen to jet fuel.

Jennifer, who was introduced in the last chapter, had wanted to become a certified yoga instructor for twenty years. It was a life goal she had continued to fail to achieve (her words). She put it down in her outcome statement. Initially, she thought it was silly to do. But once she put in writing, she took the steps to accomplish it. At the age of 56, while her third agency was expanding from 25 people to 75 people, she also became a certified yoga instructor. The mind and its chemistry don't differentiate between success on a personal goal and success in a business goal. The chemical response and dopamine release are the same. By reframing something she had long considered a failure as a success, dopamine was released and the brain functioned differently and could view events and other goals differently.

As a business owner, you need success and optimism to run a world-class business. But that success won't always be in your business. We know that. If you're firing on all cylinders, macro and micro-economic headwinds can turn a great quarter into a lousy one and drive depression. That's why the personal aspect of life must be part of your business plan.

But here's the problem. If you write an outcome statement based on your past personal, professional, or business performance, you're not going to change a thing. To change, you need to transform the way the future can look. Changing your way of viewing the future will change the way you *approach* the future. And that approach will begin in the next moment. The new approach is a vision of the future and only requires small steps now.

If you've always wanted to take five weeks off from the business, or if you've always wanted to invest in real estate, or you always wanted to earn a doctorate, and it's never occurred as a real-world possibility, then take the first step to changing the way that situation occurs by placing it in your outcome statement.

This isn't magic. There's plenty of brain science associated with this process and I've seen it work repeatedly. I can't say it strongly enough: if you start with yourself, it isn't a selfish move. You need to be healthy so you can lead your company by example: healthy employees, healthy customer service, healthy pipelines, healthy revenue, and healthy profits.

Through my experience in coaching business owners, I've seen that twelve quarters (three years) is just the right amount of time to see with a realistic lens. It's not too close, like a fist in your eye demanding your attention tomorrow, nor is it too far away, way off in the future, like trying to take a good picture of Mars with your iPhone (I know, I know, they're probably only a few years from having that capability at Apple…) the point is, to see something at just the right depth with just the right lens, well, our minds seem to be able to get a three year plan just about right. We don't try to do too much, nor too little. If we accomplish some of those three-year goals in 18 months, fine, so be it, and if it takes us right up to the 36-month mark, that's okay too.

World-Class Metrics For A World-Class You

Now that you've written your Outcome Statement, let's go over some metrics that you might consider holding yourself accountable to hit. These metrics are based on habits of other world-class leaders.

BMI: Percentage of body fat

Ability to run (distance) in (time)

Number of hours or distance exercise per week

Number of books to read per month or quarter

Number of classes or lessons taken per year or practice hours in a new skill

Days of vacation per year (actual vacation taken, Monday to Friday!)

Number of days on weekend doing no work

Number of dates with significant other per month

Percentage of children's activities attended

Hours spent with children per week – no cell phone on

Industry Expert Interviews And Case Studies:

Mario Raia

I received my master's degree in accounting from Brigham Young University (BYU). After I graduated, I worked with what is now Ernst & Young. After some time, I transitioned from that into a more local/ regional firm. Next, I started my own practice and grew it. Eventually, I sold my CPA practice off and began doing management development work for *Fortune*®100 companies.

Microsoft® was my biggest client. I worked with their executive and management development group. I worked with Intel, Ingersoll Rand, and other multinational companies, traveling all over the world. The managers who hired me to do these gigs said, "We don't quite understand it, but when they come back from you, they *think better*. We like that." I'd get a group of a couple dozen managers and work with them for a few days, and then they'd be off and that was it. I wouldn't have any other interaction with them. It was all right, but I never saw how their story ended. Eventually, I got tired of the travel, and I missed working with small to medium-sized businesses, because you can make a big difference very quickly. I wanted to work with my clients for a while, see them develop, and see how the story ended.

I looked around for about four or five years for a system that had a solid structure for coaching and also included the use of key performance indicators as guides. I was looking for a system that would help me deliver and track great KPIs for my clients.

Most of my clients did have KPIs, but we were using spreadsheets. We needed those KPIs so much that we had put them together with duct tape and coat hangers and chewing gum. I looked at probably at least a dozen other systems out there that offered KPIs, and they could do them monthly, quarterly, and annually, but they couldn't do them weekly. The problem is, KPIs must be reviewed weekly. If you're in the second week of the month, and you have a KPI that isn't behaving like it should, you have time to fix it. But if you have a monthly KPI check-in, by the time you catch the problem, you're already into the next month, and it has taken six or eight weeks to have a discussion, when you could have fixed something right away.

You want to be able to make course corrections quickly, in the middle of the month, and end up with some great numbers at the end of the month– every month.

Additionally, KPIs help my clients clarify where to put their management time and gives them a focus. The other thing about KPIs is when they're done properly, KPIs roll up into the strategic plan. So, your KPIs are getting you to your one-year goal, your three-year goals, and it all maps out.

Business is like apples and oranges. You have all this activity that you're doing, that's the apples, and the oranges are the financial results. In many businesses, it's really difficult to attach activity to results. They're two completely different things. KPIs and the Catipult system are like a bridge, they glue the two together. So, when I discovered Catipult, I said, "Yes! Finally, somebody has put together a system that gives us the KPIs we need, based on our input."

I've often observed that every business has three main functions. There's a sales and marketing function, an operational function, and a finance and administration function. Business travels across those three functions. You market, you sell something, you produce goods or deliver a service, then you send a bill and collect it, and the money comes in the door. It's a simple, linear process. If you want to speed the throughput of the business up, two things need to happen.

Number one, each process needs to be effective. Then, you need to find the weakest link in your chain of processes and fix that weakest link. I always ask: "How many weak links are there in a chain?" Well, obviously, there's only one. So that provides a point of focus.

The reason that's important is because anytime you make an improvement in that weakest link, it automatically hits the bottom line at the same time.

Next, we typically tell ourselves we need to improve our business in three areas. Everyone needs to improve by 10 percent, and if everyone improves by 10 percent, our bottom line goes up by 10 percent, right? Wrong. In reality, that does not happen, because anytime I change my sales and marketing it reverberates, it affects my operations, it affects my finance and administration. So, in the name of improving my business, when I try to improve *everything at once*, I create chaos in my business. And that's why it's so terribly difficult for businesses to improve. So, by focusing on the single biggest constraint of the business and synchronizing the other functional areas to that constraint, you're able to create an environment where you really are improving your business.

Every business has a constraint, they have to. Otherwise, mathematically, you'd have infinite profit. Apple is close, but they're not quite there! So, in other words, you want to design where you want your constraint, because it becomes a pivot point of managing the entire system, and you decide what you want your throughput to be by managing *from the constraint* of your business.

Catipult enables us to make sure that people are playing nicely in the sandbox throughout the organizational functions. They've got to have measurable targets, and it allows us to minimize chaos.

I was working with one of my clients who already had KPIs, but as we did the organizational design, and began to put roles and responsibilities into Catipult, we saw where the clog was, and we realized that their biggest constraint was in product development. It became so obvious, it hit the owner, *bam,* right in the face. They needed to hire for a certain high-skill position. They already had one employee in that position, and adding a second one would be costly. But when we crunched the numbers, we realized that the business was losing mid-five figures for every month the owner chose not to add a second person in that role; in other words, adding that person would increase the bottom line by roughly $500,000 per year.

The clarity we got on what specific role and responsibility he needed to hire for, and what that would do to help the business move to the next level, came to us in an instant. I had been doing coaching with this particular client for about a year; we were making good progress and getting things done. But this was a quantum leap we attained, just by setting them up on Catipult.

CHAPTER 5:
MISSION, VISION,
AND VALUES

Note to mission, vision, and values experts: Don't skip this chapter! If you're a Mission, Vision and Values statements geek and have worked hard on them, look for the Masterclass at the end of the chapter to hone your skills one more notch.

As I mentioned in the previous chapter, there are four statements every business needs. This chapter addresses the trifecta of Mission, Vision, and Values. It isn't uncommon for people to misunderstand how to write and use Mission, Vision, and Values statements. Oftentimes, people get confused between mission and vision statements. It's not unusual for people to pick values that sound solid or trendy without examining whether they or their businesses are functioning within those values or whether they are merely aspirational. World-class companies must differentiate between them. Mission,

Vision, and Values statements ought to be as simple as possible, and tied to who you are as an owner. They should be complimentary to your outcome statement. You will use these three to create a common language for your leadership team, so, much like the Seven Business Drivers with common language, they should be easy to understand. Common language creates shorthand to remind people of what's important. It builds teamwork and brings focus to each day.

Let's take them one at a time.

MISSION: *Why are you doing the things you do, making the things you make, serving the people you serve?*

The mission is *why* you do things. When you are writing a mission statement, think about the concept of 'your why'. Simon Sinek has a great book called *Start with Why*. I highly recommend that as a resource. Why does your company exist? Why do you show up every day? Why do you care? While writing your mission statement, focus more on the Why question.

Next, we'll discuss vision, and you'll see the difference between these two critical elements.

VISION: *What will be different? What impact are we making?*

When writing the vision statement, you need to think about what impact you are going to have. What impact will your business have on your community, your employees and ultimately, your customers? That vision sets you apart. It is what really gets people excited. There's a proverb that says, "Where there is no vision, the people perish." A company is just made up of people, right? So, if you don't have a vision for your company, it's not going to do as well as other companies in your space, companies that do have that vision, and are able to rally their teams around it. So, if "Why" is the question for the mission statement, what is the question to ponder in producing a vision statement? The answer is: "To what end?" What is your picture of a transformed world? How do you see the world differently in your vision of the ideal future? You may need to write several paragraphs down, then distill them into a sentence or six key words.

VALUES: *How will you get there? How will you behave as you travel toward that future?*

A values statement is the third statement that all world-class companies have. Values are very important and often not used as they should be. As a matter of fact, I've coached a lot of companies and owners who didn't have a values statement at all. They weren't sure what it was or even what the purpose of listing out their values was. Think about your values as setting a tone for your culture. What kind of culture do you want to create? You create the culture by developing a values rubric and then hiring the people who already embody those values.

One of the things entrepreneurs value most is creativity. When you're starting a company, you need people who are going to bring their creative juices to solve the big problem of launching a company and making it successful. Now, I guarantee you (though I cannot know this for a fact) that creativity is probably not a value they're hiring for a lot at most McDonald's® franchises. If McDonald's were to hire me to work on the grill, they would get 25 different burgers for the next 25 different customers who order a burger. I'd throw avocado on one, a slice of pineapple on the next, habanero salsa or a fried egg or who knows what... Some of them will be delicious. Some will probably be awful. But that's not what they want. They don't want creativity. What they want is consistency and reliability. They want a team who can produce (not re-create) a burger repeatedly and do it to the company's precise specifications every time. So, hiring for creativity is probably not a core value for McDonald's, at least at the grill level.

What do you need in your company? What are those values? Take some time on this, it's important. Only then can you create that rubric and make sure that you're hiring for it. Yes, you can even begin firing against that rubric. Because when people don't embody the values you need, it becomes a cancer throughout the organization.

Values are all about how you do what you do to get there, or, as the Boeing values (see below) state: "How we act." If you say that you value integrity, for example, that might mean "We'll get there without breaking the law or violating moral, ethical, or spiritual principles, even if we could get away with it." Values are not as tricky as you may think, because they manifest themselves in behaviors. It's easy to check for yourself if your values are in practice or only aspirational. For example, I say I value lifelong learning. So, do I read at least one book a month, or not? Do I take classes to learn more about my industry, or not? How does what I say I value manifest itself in my behavior?

This is not to say you shouldn't include a values statement that's aspirational. Perhaps you just build an outcome statement that says, "The year is 2027 and I am spending every weekend with my family." Now you want to include the values word "family-oriented" although at this time you're not yet living that value. That's okay, because now that it is in your outcome statement, your new value is no longer aspirational, it's in the beginning phases of a practiced behavior.

Boeing: here's a snippet from Boeing's webpage on Values, which, frankly, is a bit wordy overall, but this bit is excellent:

> "How we act: Lead on safety, quality, integrity, and sustainability. In everything we do and in all aspects of our business, we will make safety our top priority, strive for first-time quality, hold ourselves to the highest ethical standards, and continue to support a sustainable future."[5]

I don't know about you, but if I purchased or hired a private jet for speed and efficiency, I'd still be glad to know that Boeing didn't say "faster" or "more efficient" first. Even though these are the benefits you get from your private jet, knowing that safety and quality are their top priorities is important. What good is delivering airborne speed if it isn't safe? NetJets, too, lists "an unwavering commitment to safety" as the first thing they look for in a new employee.[6]

With all of these: Mission, Vision, and Values, you must also ask yourself: Can people say them? Are they easy to remember and memorize? Maybe you think that you have done all that great work on your offsite last year, as you spent two days with your leadership team reviewing and polishing your mission, vision and values statements. Well, if so, that's great, because it means you can put it to the test right now. Go to one of your executives, a mid-level manager, and an hourly employee, and see how many of them can repeat the mission, vision, and values statement. Can they also tell you how the company is doing those things in simple, practical terms?

If they can't, it's time to simplify. Get some outside perspective on it if you must.

Catipult's Mission, Vision, And Values

To offer another example and to allow you to get to know me a bit better, here are the mission, vision, and values statements for my company:

Mission: Catipult's mission is to help the global community of business owners become healthier and more valuable.

Vision: Catipult's vision is to change the trajectory of 1,000,000 businesses through the power of scalable technology and a large community of expert coaches who, thanks to Catipult, are free to be themselves without the time-consuming burden of finding clients, creating programs, and administering those programs. We believe that increasing the success of business owners will have a positive impact on the families those businesses support and the economy.

Values: Catipult is a global organization. Our values are focused on the following five characteristics: maintaining a global worldview, putting people first, and holding each other accountable while being innovative and driven.

Masterclass

If you're an old hand at Mission, Vision and Values statements, take on this additional challenge: Try to make three PowerPoint® slides (one for mission, one for vision, and one for values) with a single, memorable image which depicts your message in metaphor, and no more than six words per slide.

Here is my example, based on Catipult's longer statements above:

(Mission) Helping healthy owners grow valuable companies.

(Vision) One million owners experiencing freedom.

(Values) Accountable people, driving innovation globally.

If you can do this, you'll notice that you're now asking each person in your company to know only 18 words or fewer by heart. We did ours (in the example above) in 16 words. That's shorter than the Pledge of Allegiance, so you know it can be memorized.

Industry Expert Interview And Case Study:

Set Up Speed Uncovers Core Values Discussion Early

We're working on a partnership with a fractional COO group called Wolf's Edge Integrators. Fractional COOs typically go in as a part-time COO to help the business owner get their executive team in order. Once they build the team and hire their replacement, they step out.

Last month I went with a fractional integrator to have dinner with a prospective client. It was on August 23rd. The client made the decision to move forward on Friday, August 25th. On Monday, August 28th, we onboarded their executive team.

The next week, on September 7th, we did a core values session. As we started working on discovering their core values, one of the leadership team members said, "I'm probably not going to be very popular for saying this, but I have to. Right now, we have very little team trust and we have an awful lot of people stabbing each other in the back. So this whole exercise is kind of bullshit."

I paused for something like 60 to 90 seconds, to let that marinate in the silence, and then I asked, "Does anyone want to disagree with

---

what she just said?" No one disagreed. It started this really great discussion that wound up leading us to discover the true core values forty-five minutes later. It also helped the owner realize that he's got a culture problem ... and he's a huge part of that problem. We figured out this major issue within two weeks of starting to work with this client.

This enabled the owner to do some reflection and self-actualization type work that his fractional COO and I are going to coach him through. And as he's putting the right people in the right seats, now he's bringing on people who are complementary to him, not like him.

A lot of my clients absolutely love the fact that instead of doing full-day quarterly sessions, we're doing half-day quarterly sessions with a six-week tactical check-in. They really struggled with going three months without the help of a coach and a facilitator. Having that six-week check-in keeps them super focused with their action items and makes sure that they're not going down a rabbit hole when a crisis pops up. They're no longer finding themselves suddenly at the end of the quarter and realizing, "Shoot, we didn't get anything done." Yes, there's a little more frequency, but the meetings aren't as long.

I found out with one company that half of the people on the executive team are dog owners. They were really excited about not having to be at work at 7:30 in the morning to attend a long meeting because it upset their dog's routine. It really does start with you– and your employees! So now, they can do that morning walk with the dog and keep their routine, get to work at nine, do the half-day session, and still have the remainder of the day to get all their work done. And they're accomplishing more in that half-day than they did in a full-day session.

Chapter 6: Focused, World-Class KPI Targets

In this chapter, we're going to cover the concept of key performance indicators (KPIs). Companies have been using KPIs for decades to define success indicators and measure progress against them. Typically, they are used to measure the operational areas of business performance and are often associated with industry standards or internal expectations of process outcomes and not always tied to the company's strategic objectives.

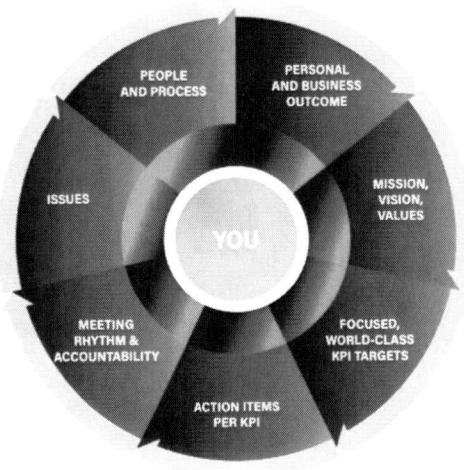

Several schools of thought use KPIs only for weekly scorecards and relegate strategic decisions to be communicated in the form of goals and major rocks necessary to accomplish those goals. Their approach isn't really that uncommon. Even companies not using that system or others like it tend to place the strategic initiatives on a slide deck and assign major projects to further those objectives.

The major challenge with this for business owners is that as they pass along the responsibility for those rocks, they aren't associated with any clear, strategic, measurable reason for doing them. This often leads to internal disassociation of the strategic plan from the operational KPIs the company uses to run itself.

This disassociation is dangerous, costly, and confusing. It also doesn't scale well into the organization. How could it? Rocks are written in long form and slideware isn't easily delivered to the company. The company is naturally more focused on what is being measured, so when the rocks it establishes aren't tied to a company's operations, they often aren't given the focus they need. This is a primary reason why CEOs of major corporations—those who most consider world-class operations—don't use this methodology.

You shouldn't, either, as this type of thinking can lead your company quickly into a ditch. The biggest struggle I have with systems that don't tie the activity layer—the initiatives/rocks that need to be done—to strategic KPIs is that it gives owners a false sense of strategic direction and operational success.

Even more frustrating is that strategic KPIs are not well-known, and most owners don't discover them until they begin to consider a transition of some kind like selling the company. This is a much different situation than owners of funded technology start-ups experience. When funded, a start-up CEO knows the endgame: they are building a company to sell or take public. Because of this, they are exposed from day one to the concept of strategic KPIs making sure the company is being designed to hit them.

What would it be like to run a company in which everything—and I mean everything—that was being done was tied to a measurable, objective reason for doing it? What would it be like if your rocks were tied to strategic KPIs that were immutable and guaranteed to give you more time back, higher valuations, increased retention, lower costs of borrowing and, above all, less stress?

The answer, of course, is "that would be amazing." That's what you're going to experience in this chapter. It's a methodology that guarantees you success and makes problem solving incredibly fast, reduces meeting times, and aligns teams almost effortlessly. Let's get started.

The Six CORE KPIs That RUN Every Company In The World

Yes, it is true. These KPIs are running your company whether you know about them or not. While there are certainly a few more strategic KPIs, if you did nothing else but manage to the core six and delegated the rest, you'd be far ahead of your competition.

The graphic below shows the core six. Knowing these core six KPIs and using them to guide the actions and initiatives in your company will save you a lot of headaches and make your company a highly stable and sought-after world-class organization, which ultimately gives you want you want most as an owner – options and freedom.

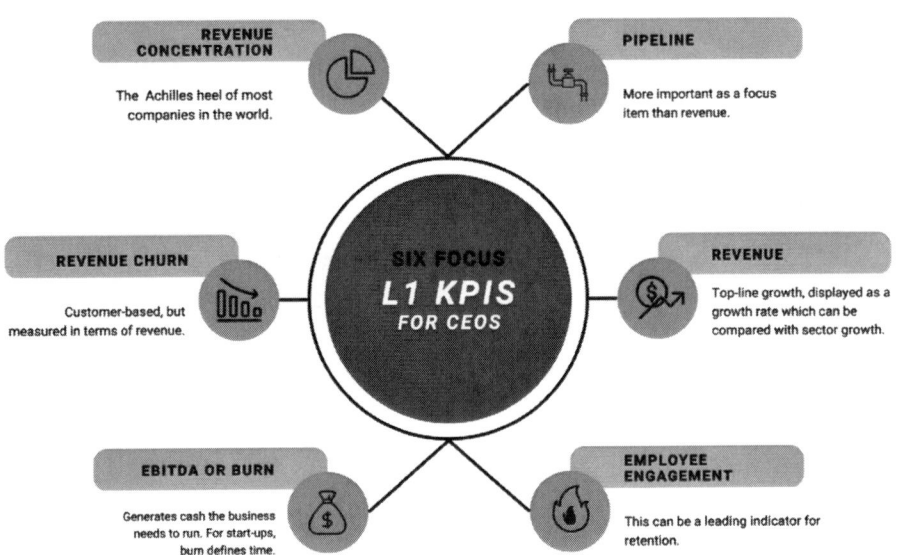

The Core Six And The Formulas Behind Them

KPI #1: Employee Engagement Score

The CEO or owner needs to keep one main thing in mind: you should always have an eye on this as a KPI, but you don't need to get in depth on the details with your head of Human Resources unless there's a problem.

Employee engagement is a leading indicator of turnover and, most likely, problems with your managers. Employees often leave a company because they have a problem with their direct manager.

Having regular reporting on this metric will help you address issues before they arise. There are many different solutions for getting this metric. A few of them are listed below. At Catipult, we recommend Tiny Pulse® for its simplicity, ease-of-use, and price. If you don't have a solution in place in your company, consider getting one immediately. As an owner, it's best to have advanced warning than surprise departures.

These days, most employee experience solutions claim to have real-time reporting. Gone are the days when your HR manager had to wait weeks for surveys to come back in.

Qualtrics: Qualtrics promises "a holistic view of every lifecycle touchpoint … from recruitment to exit."

Gallup: Known historically for their surveys, Gallup promises surveys with "the right questions to get to the heart of what your employees need."

Lattice: Lattice claims to "help companies identify what keeps employees engaged."

There are many other software solutions, apps, and companies ready to support your needs at a variety of price points, so don't say "that's for the megaliths, the *Fortune* 500 companies." Remember, being world-class isn't about size.

KPI #2: Revenue Concentration In One Customer: Under 20 Percent

Remember Kevin, the guy who lost three years of retirement resolving a revenue concentration issue? Because he had too much of his revenue from one customer, the bank determined the value of his business was only $65 million, not the $100 million it should have been by any other measure.

That's because revenue concentration over 20 percent is a vulnerability. What if you lost that one big fish? Would you have to lay off employees? Take on more debt to keep operating until your sales catch up with the revenue churn? Put it this way: if it's too much risk for a bank, it's too much risk for you.

One thing to watch out for is the idea that you may be sending multiple invoices to one customer, and your team could be counting it as multiple customers. Imagine that you own a carpet cleaning business. You got your start doing residential jobs, but one day, you land a deal to clean the carpets and wax floors for a regional franchise group with sixteen locations, where each franchisee pays their own invoice, but the contract is negotiated by the group.

When calculating revenue concentration, be careful not to think of these as multiple customers! If they collectively amount to 30 percent of your business' revenue, and if the group decided to go with one of your competitors the next year, it's still a loss of 30 percent of your revenue in one shot. Rule of thumb: If you're vulnerable to losing all of it in one shot for any reason, for the purposes of accuracy in measuring your revenue concentration, it must be tracked as one account with multiple sub-accounts.

Does this mean that you shouldn't go for it when given the opportunity to increase your revenue by 400 percent with one customer overnight? Not necessarily but think carefully about committing to a contract that will put you in this kind of vulnerable situation. Businesses have been bankrupted by losing those kinds of contracts.

Licensing Deals Are A Concentration Of Revenue

It was Valentine's Day in 2011. I was in my garage at 7 p.m. on the phone with my contact at IBM®. She was at dinner with her husband. I was trying to go to dinner with my wife. I had to renegotiate a licensing arrangement my company had with IBM or else a new investor would pull the $19 million in capital that was already in escrow. My entire company was at stake. Without that infusion, we'd have been shuttering our doors in three weeks. The problem I had to solve: we had built a product that was entirely dependent on a core piece of IBM technology and IBM had just made a global price change that would have forced us to increase our product price tenfold just to maintain our current 30 percent margins. Our market wouldn't stand for it.

Luckily, IBM is a great company to work for and my contact there negotiated the new terms of our agreement during her romantic dinner with her husband. Even then, the venture capital firm insisted that we use its funds to create our own core technology and end the IBM license in 18 months. We did just that.

Distribution Deals Are A Concentration Of Revenue

The best form of learning is experience. In one of my other companies, we had made the strategic decision to sell our product exclusively through resellers and not direct to the customer. Many companies do this as resellers offset many costs that a company would have to incur when servicing a customer directly. Many resellers work with distributors. Distributors create an easy access point for companies like mine to reach and manage resellers. Rather than having 2,000 individual resellers to manage, companies can often have two or three main distributors they use who then, in turn, sell to and manage the resellers.

Strategically, owners need to think of these distribution deals as concentrations of revenue. After all, a distributor can cancel your contract and cut you off from its resellers. Or, your competitor can become overly aggressive and target you within the distributor by offering its sales team enormous incentives NOT to sell your product.

Yes, the latter happened to my company. Without naming names, my company was the "David" to an industry "Goliath" who made the strategic decision that it may be cheaper to run us out of business than to buy us. Competitors don't announce these things; you just find them out over time. In this one case, I was curious why our sales through a prime distributor had stopped. I called to order my own product and the salesperson at the other end of the line did everything they could to sell me the competitor's product instead.

What made this even more concerning is that I had paid well into the six-figures for sponsorship with this distributor, which meant they should be at least selling my product to people who asked for it. After more investigation and some "insider" calls with promises of anonymity, we discovered that Goliath was offering negative profit incentives (selling their product at a loss) in any deal that involved us. They also spent a few million to my six figures on other sales incentives within this distributor.

Fortunately, our concentration of revenue was not more than 20 percent in this one distributor and the impact on our business, while frustrating, was negligible. The strategy to balance sales across multiple distributors saved us from a world of hurt.

Markets Can Be A Concentration Of Revenue

Prior to COVID, specialization in one market was considered a great strategy. Not anymore. It's better to specialize in an area of expertise and with a product that could have application to a few markets. Many companies who provided services and products to industries deemed "non-essential" during the pandemic went out of business. Their specialization was also their demise as the time to re-tool marketing or even product direction wasn't sufficient when the market changed so quickly.

What Is Concentration Of Revenue?

Ultimately, as the examples above prove, the definition spans to include all sources your revenue is dependent upon.

Watch this metric closely.

Strategically Applying This Metric With Your Outcome Statement

One owner we worked with had a goal of exiting the company in three years with $100 million in revenue and 20 percent EBITDA. To achieve that goal, we put in a plan of action items (our version of rocks) across multiple departments to support that three-year outcome.

Midway through the process, the ultimate test came for the CEO: she won a major contract that put them above the $100 million mark. Ordinarily, this is a good thing. However, this contract was with a *Fortune* 10 company who also did business with her most likely acquirers. It also changed her concentration of revenue to 35 percent for one customer and 70 percent in just three customers.

Achieving the $100 million revenue target devalued the company and made it less stable. It also put at risk the EBITDA target as the company was now at the whim of three companies who could—and did—like to negotiate price.

In other words, not all revenue is good revenue. At least this CEO knew what her world concentration needed to be and made an informed decision to take a risk and bring on the new client. Most owners aren't so fortunate and make these decisions blindly without knowing what impact they have on the core value and stability of the business. This is why managing these world-class KPIs is essential.

Review

Formula: Revenue from largest client divided by total revenue. Ideal answer: under 20 percent. If the answer is over 20 percent, you are carrying unnecessary risk.

Recommended Reporting Rhythm: Considerations may include number of tickets weekly/monthly or new clients onboarded. If you have a high volume of clients coming and going every week, track it weekly. If you have fewer than 50 every three months, you may only want to check up on this quarterly.

Note: *If you are in retail, you may not worry about this as much as monitoring the average ticket on a weekly basis compared to the same week in the previous year. However, even some retail places may have corporate accounts, perhaps taking care of a municipal snow plow fleet, so just because you're in retail doesn't necessarily mean you don't have a revenue concentration problem.*

My Rhythm: How often will your team report on this KPI? _____

KPI #3: Revenue Churn At Net Positive

Remember Melissa, who ran a training company and was only tracking customers gained and customers lost? Revenues had flattened over the years and nothing they seemed to do was able to boost growth rates. The problem wasn't with the product, it was with one metric: Churn. They had no idea how much revenue was leaving annually, as they only measured churn by new customers coming in against old customers leaving. Melissa knew her business was stagnant, but she didn't have a good handle on what was happening.

After discussing Revenue Concentration, Churn becomes a little easier to think about.

Scenario One: Betty has a million-dollar business serving 40 clients, averaging $25,000 per year. In 2024, Betty's marketing and sales department feels that they killed it, because she's gained fifteen clients. Even though the team struggles to onboard more than one new client per month, they lose only three. Her client churn is net +12. Great, right?

But when Betty realizes that the fifteen clients her sales team gained an average of $10,000 in revenue per year, and then realizes the three she lost were averaging $75,000 per year, she realizes the company is in trouble. Her people are scrambling to serve the additional clients, each new client has about half a dozen frustrated people calling with questions all day long, while the revenue churn is -$75,000. Betty may not have Revenue Concentration problems, but she does have churn issues.

Scenario Two: On the flip side, Joe also has a million-dollar business serving 40 clients, averaging $25,000 per year. In 2024, he loses six customers averaging $10,000 per year, while gaining three customers averaging $50,000 per year. Joe has net negative customer churn (-3 total customers) but net positive revenue churn (+$90,000 revenue). Joe's having a great life. His revenue grew by 9 percent while the industry average was 5 percent. His team is focused on serving fewer clients, they're getting fewer complaints from clients who can barely afford their service, and the largest client he gained is bringing him a revenue of $100,000, so he's not too worried about concentration. His revenue concentration in one customer is a little higher than it was in 2023, climbing to 9.2 percent. He lost more clients than he gained, but his revenue churn is a positive number.

Formula: instead of focusing on customers gained minus customers lost, pay attention to revenue gained minus revenue lost. Ideal answer: gaining positive revenue and positive number of clients, however, since eliminating clients who create more hassle than they're worth on the lower end can also be a positive thing, depending on your circumstances, you might consider positive revenue churn and negative client churn to be your ideal situation.

Rhythms: Again, the frequency with which this should be monitored depends on the volume of clients coming and going, whether it needs to be on a weekly, monthly or quarterly basis.

My Rhythm: I need my team to report on Revenue Churn, _____

KPI #4: Pipeline Calculated To Achieve The World-Class Growth Percentage Target

Revenue is important, but a focus on pipeline is more useful than top line revenue for the CEO to track on a regular basis. CEOs who track pipeline routinely are more likely to achieve their revenue numbers. That said, the formula for tracking pipeline is often misunderstood which leads to stalls in growth.

In a meeting, a client had decided that they needed to discuss a pullback in marketing expenses. Their pipeline was already 5x greater than their revenue goals and they didn't need to spend any more money trying to get business it was afraid it couldn't handle. Their goal was to double their topline revenue in three years and they felt they had the pipeline coverage to do just that.

After hitting the pause button for a moment, we reviewed their formula. Unfortunately for them, it was way off...by 2x and they not only were going to miss their growth target by a light year, but they were also looking at a second consecutive year of stagnant growth. The problem was simple to fix. The company wasn't calculating the time to close, and percentage of deals won or their outcome statement into the formula. When those were added, the numbers showed they need to double their pipeline to hit their outcome statement target in 18 months. Rather than cutting marketing, they continued it and built the pipeline to where it needed to be. Like magic, they achieved their outcome statement goal right on plan.

The moral of this story is that stagnant growth may not have anything to do with your product, team, or strategy. It could simply be a formula error.

To calculate pipeline, follow these steps:

1. Determine the time it takes a deal to go from the top of the pipeline to the closed/won stage.
2. Review your financial model for your three-year outcome.
3. Based on the time it takes to close a deal, consider the revenue that is expected when a deal closes.
4. Determine your close rate percentage.
5. Based on this data, calculate the pipeline your company needs to meet its revenue target.

For example, Acme company sells large projects that take six months to close. They close 10 percent of the deals in their pipeline. The revenue target based on their three-year plan calls for $1 Million in revenue in Q2. This means the beginning pipeline on January 1 (first day of Q1) needs to be $10 MM to close $1 MM by June 30th. If current performance is below the recommended target, then create an issue to create a plan to achieve the target. To do so, your sales team can increase their pipeline by 1) bidding more jobs or 2) closing a higher percentage. That's the simple part... and it's easy to oversimplify!

If you've found that your pipeline isn't currently positioned to make World-Class growth outcomes by the end of three years, consider the average sales cycle: what's the average lag time between delivering a bid to securing revenue? If you discover that you aren't putting out enough bids, and recognize that your sales cycle averages 12 months, you may need to increase your bids even more for a while– and even then, it could take 12 months for your pipeline to catch up with the quotas you've set for growth. Owners who uncover pipeline challenges may need to be patient as their team ramps up marketing and sales activity for the duration of a full sales cycle… or you can ask yourself:

How can we speed up our sales cycle in the short term? Upsell a current project?

The shortest sales cycle in the world is hamburgers. The salesperson has 5 seconds to upsell me to a full meal, a milkshake, or whatever, and then I walk out again. I may be hungry for another hamburger in five hours, although I might opt for a salad next time.

The longest sales cycles could be government contracts for paving a road, selling houses or cars, or even selling a college education. On the flip side, when you're in the market for a car, you're in the market for about as long as you are when you want a hamburger. The point is, there are two ways to look at that sales cycle: it may be three to seven years between automobile purchases, but when the time comes, you need transportation urgently.

When you begin to look at pipeline and growth percentages, don't forget that your pipeline calculations need to compensate for negative revenue churn. If your growth is 5 percent above industry standards, but you've forgotten to account for negative revenue churn, you probably don't have world-class growth. In fact, you might be shrinking.

Finally, a good pipeline requires a good CRM system so that you can develop rhythms and make sure to follow up with people even if they're going to be on the longer end of your sales cycle. If your sales team isn't following up, you could be losing 90 percent of the opportunities they opened in the first place. A rule of thumb for your pipeline KPI is to work smarter, not harder.

Rhythm: It depends on how far you are behind your current pipeline target. The CEO needs to track it monthly, while your Chief Sales Officer may want to track it (and other related KPIs) on a weekly basis so he or she can provide interventions for the sales team.

KPI #5: EBITDA (Earnings Before Interest, Tax, Depreciation And Amortization)

Alternative KPI For Startups: BURN

After all that work generating revenue, and focusing on KPIs related to revenue that aren't the top-line number, like Pipeline, Churn and Customer Concentration, well…

What's the point of having revenue if you're spending more than you bring in? Tracking your Earnings Before Interest, Tax, Depreciation and Amortization (EBITDA) or Burn is essential. Each department may have expenses they're responsible for, and the CEO can ask his or her executives to create KPIs for themselves which are geared toward increasing revenue while decreasing expenditures, but EBITDA is the key marker that every CEO needs to track monthly.

Burn: When startup companies are in pre-revenue phase, burn is the alternative KPI that indicates how much runway you have left before that revenue airplane needs to lift off– or before you're going to have to give up more ownership to additional investors.

Know your bottom line just as precisely as your top line.

Rhythm: Monthly.

KPI #6: Top-Line Revenue Growth by Percentage (And Compared To Sector Growth)

World-class CEOs usually discuss growth as a percentage and aren't fixated on the actual revenue number. That's best left for the head of sales if you have one. There's a reason for this: When you focus your attention on your growth rate, you're more likely to compare your growth rate to that of your industry.

As I mentioned previously, the opportunity to grow and shrink simultaneously is a normal function of business. If your company's revenue is growing slower than your market is growing, then your business is technically shrinking.

Acme (name changed intentionally) was growing a healthy 10 percent per year. The owner was happy and so was the team. Whenever the owner talked about growth, he mentioned it in relation to his company's previous year's performance. This was a big mental mistake. As a CEO, it is important to measure your growth in relation to the growth of the market you serve, not last year's performance. Have your CFO focus on that metric.

Acme's market was exploding. Over the last three years, the market for products like Acme's has tripled. Acme had only grown 10 percent. Was the company growing or shrinking? It was shrinking. Acme's competitors were serving the demand and devouring market share. When this was brought to the CEO's attention, things began to change…quickly.

There are many markets today that are experiencing this phenomenon. One of them was the organic chocolate market. For years, it was dominated by a few players who enjoyed plenty of shelf space in grocery stores. As we've all seen, shelf space (a great metaphor for market share) has gotten crowded. Companies that once enjoyed 40 percent of the space available for that category of product have been diminished to ten percent or less, in some cases, as they failed to create new products.

What Is World-Class Growth?

With this KPI, world-class is defined as your mindset. As the owner, always consider your growth rate in comparison with that of your industry's. A good rule is to then try to exceed that growth rate by as much as you think you can. Growing in pace with industry growth is simply managing inflation. Growing above that number is real growth and that adds value and stability to your company.

How to calculate growth rate: current value minus previous value. Take the difference and divide by previous value. Multiply by 100.

Example: Wanda's Match Factory pipeline indicates she's on track to sell $500,000 in 2024, (that's a lot of matchsticks, folks) and she sold $464,000 the year in 2023.

$500,000 (current value) - $464,000 (previous value) = 36,000.

$36,000 (difference) / $464,000 (previous value) = .0775 (x100) = 7.75 percent. If the market for matches grew 2 percent during that year, Wanda's doing great. If it grew 20 percent, not so much.

Decision Making Methodology

Now that we've covered the core six KPIs, let's look at how to use them for making decisions quickly. This next section will cover how owners should approach KPIs with their teams, how your teams may react and finally, how to accomplish rapid decision-making with this system.

An Owner's Approach To A Strategic KPI System

As we dial this into actionable implementation strategies, it's important to understand that context around a world-class system like this will change. To experience this, let's look at this speedometer-like diagram, which describes a world-class KPI with a maximum threshold for concentration of revenue in one customer at 20 percent.

There's a line that says 15 percent, another that says 20 percent, indicating the target, and a third red line that says 35 percent, which represents a customer's current concentration of revenue. 20 percent is the target for every company, regardless of industry. The 15 percent difference between the world-class standard and their actual performance cost them $35,000,000 in valuation. If the CEO had known this one metric earlier, he would have managed his company much differently.

What about the 15 percent line? If the company only had 15 percent of its revenue coming from one source, then it would outperform the world-class metric of 20 percent. That would be great, and the company could even shoot for 13 percent if they wanted, but the 20 percent maximum target would not change: it's the number that matters when you attempt to determine the value of your company. Anything below 20 percent is great, above, not so much. Strategic KPIs, therefore, are often static rubrics to continually measure performance against. This makes managing for owners much easier.

KPIs Must Associate With Your Outcome

Don't look at KPIs as industry standards. World-class companies aren't just running on industry standards, they're running on their own goals and metrics that often exceed standards. Most standards, especially non-quality related ones, are based on average performance of the specific class. If you want to be world-class, then meeting the average standard is not enough.

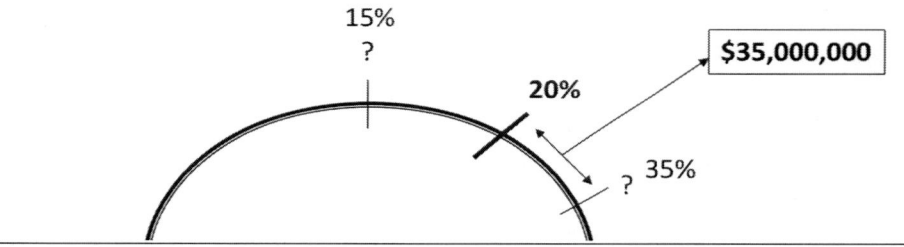

Your KPIs need to be based on your desired outcome, not industry standards. If your outcome is to sell a company, you may need to set KPIs much differently than if your outcome was to grow and/or acquire other companies. If standard employee retention for your industry is 80 percent, but you want 90 percent to achieve your goals, then 90 percent is your target.

KPIs Are Not Punitive

Here's where many CEOs fall flat with their teams. When a KPI is not achieved, they focus on the goal and say we "failed to hit the target." Don't do that. Sure, it may be true, but there is a better way to state what happened. Let's unpack this.

Scenario: KPI: Blue Widgets to Create Each Month. **Target** 100. **Actual**: 74

You have two ways to communicate with the team.

Option 1: "Team, our target is 100 and we failed to hit it! We're having a meeting to figure out what is stopping us from making 100 blue widgets. Come prepared with a plan for 100 and why we are failing."

Option 2: "Team, our target is 100 and we accomplished building 74 blue widgets. While it's short of our target, we just need to figure out how to produce 26 more widgets per month. I know that a team who could figure out how to produce 74 widgets can certainly figure out how to produce 26 more! Let's talk on Monday!"

Which statement will have the team excited to brainstorm on Monday and which won't? As a world-class leader, your job is to manage the emotions and brain chemistry of your team. Negative energy and punitive responses don't serve your goals. Having a team solve for 26 instead of 100 will have much different results.

To truly experience the awesome speed of the KPI-managed system, you need to make sure you are communicating appropriately. Only solve for the deltas, never for the entire target. This is a very important nuance.

Let me make my point by example. One of my coaching clients had two major events unfold in the same quarter: (1) they failed to meet their quarterly EBITDA goals; and (2) learned that four major customers may not renew their contracts with their company.

Here's how our conversation unfolded:

CEO: We failed to meet our profitability targets last quarter, and unrelated to that, I learned this week that four of our major accounts are now up for review. We may lose them.

Peter: Let's look at each event separately. First, your profitability goals were not met.

CEO: Yes, that's right. We needed to be at 5 percent; we were at 2.5 percent.

Peter: Okay. How are you reacting to that news?

CEO: I'm not happy, and I communicated that to my team, and we're taking measures to get back on plan.

Peter: So, are you confident that your plan is something your business can achieve?

CEO: Yes, of course. That's why I wrote the plan.

Peter: But your company didn't meet the plan. It's somewhere else.

CEO: Right, I get what you're saying. But a company needs a plan and goals to drive toward. Without that, we'll never hit anything.

Peter: Okay. Let's talk about those four customers.

CEO: Yes, there were internal employee changes at those customers' companies, and the new people in charge are reviewing all vendors and will likely negotiate us down—again.

Peter: Several unrelated events are occurring. Let's not consider any one of them failed or assume that getting back to plan is the right thing for the company right now. Let's just look at where we are as changes that occurred may or may not be out of your control. Employee changes at your major accounts are certainly out of your control.

CEO: Okay, sure. We are at 2.5 percent profit, and we planned to be at 5 percent, and four customers may leave us or at least negotiate us down.

Peter: Other than price, what other competitive advantages does your company have that might allow it to keep the business without being price-pressured?

CEO: None—in that area. It's a commodity service. We compete on price. That's it. In this other division, we have a lot of advantages and higher profitability—around 10 percent.

Peter: Let me reflect on what I'm hearing. Your profits didn't meet plan, and you are preparing to lower your profit margins to keep four customers in your commodity, price-war-exposed business unit and expecting management to double net income to 5 percent by next quarter.

CEO: Yes, that's correct.

Peter: Given what I just restated, did your company fail to meet the plan or could the plan be faulty?

CEO: Yes, I get what you're saying. If I keep those customers—insist on keeping those customers—they'll further pressure margins. The reality of the situation is that we'll need to double our cost reduction plan to meet net income targets, but keeping those customers may reduce net income by half a point. It certainly wouldn't increase it.

Peter: Right. So, have you failed or are you and your company exactly where it should be?

CEO: It occurs that we are where we need to be. Keeping those customers doesn't make sense for the business if they continue to squeeze our profitability.

Peter: Tell me about the other business unit with 10 percent profit margins. What would it take to grow that margin contribution to something significant enough to influence overall net income?

CEO: Cash. We have cash.

Peter: *Silence. I just wait for the executive to connect all the dots.*

CEO: Okay. Here's what we need to consider: (1) the plan was wrong, not my team; (2) the business is flawed because it is overly reliant on the commodity business for revenue; (3) keeping those four customers at all costs—may cost us too much. We need to do a thorough profit and loss audit on them before choosing whether to keep them or let them go; and (4) a better path to hitting our profitability objectives may be to invest in this smaller division because it's not a commodity sale and has much higher net incomes.

Peter: That's a much different strategy than the one you described when the meeting began. What made the difference?

CEO: Well, you forced me to look at our results, not as a failure to achieve, but rather as events that needed to be investigated. Ultimately, it seems the plan is to blame because the company is out of balance. Any new plan to hit profitability targets must consider growing the profitable business units while winding ourselves out of the commodity business we've been doing for twenty years.

In the real-world example above, the CEO changed the way he viewed the plan. Did you notice the shift?

Starting perspective: Initially, the CEO believed he failed to meet the plan and had communicated that to the management team, pushing them to get back onto plan.

Transition: After removing the word "failure," the CEO then was open to the concept that perhaps the plan, not his team, was not realistic.

New vantage point: He then acknowledged that the company is on a different line (not the linear progression he planned) and that this new place is likely exactly where the company should be, given its current structure.

New vision: Once acknowledging that he was at a new point, he then changed the way the four low-margin, high-revenue customers occurred to him. His mind then went into rapid-fire mode, generating the radically new idea that he should strongly consider growing the small high-margin business at the expense of the commodity business they were in for twenty years—and possibly fire the four low-margin customers.

Positive energy hits the executive team: The CEO went back to the executive team with a new perspective. They hadn't failed. Situations occurred that prevented the plan from being met, and therefore, analysis of a new strategy was needed as a result. The goals were noble and still the target. The team was now given the freedom to explore creative avenues to increase profitability that no one had considered previously. In the linear progression model, the only possibility of achievement is the next progression, which was net income of 5 percent.

After that session, he ultimately fired one customer and spent the next three years building up the portions of his business with the 10 percent margins and ultimately grew those margins to 15 percent. That business unit happened to be cold storage. By focusing on that, he won major business from Amgen and other large pharmaceuticals. When COVID took the world by storm, he was chosen to store all the vaccines for the state of Indiana.

The concept of failure forces the mind into survival and scarcity mode. In that place, it has a harder time producing creative ideas. To get world-class speed from yourself and your team, solve the deltas, eliminate the notion of failure, and focus on the future.

That's the power of the KPI-based system. It allows you to clearly define a problem and get the best out of your team.

How Your Team Looks At KPIs

As you choose to implement this process, you'll run into some resistance. Employees and even managers tend to view KPIs as punitive. This response is likely because their limited experience with them has been, well, punitive.

KPIs are not punitive: they're simply a measurement. What your team may balk at is the accountability associated with KPIs.

I ran into a VP of Sales—we'll call him Squirmy to protect his real name—who lost his mind when the CEO implemented the Catipult process. Squirmy was asked to create KPIs for his department, arguably one of the most measurable departments in an organization. He resisted and fought the idea for four weeks. I had never seen someone squirm like this. Finally, he produced some numbers that included the standard quarterly revenue targets and delivered a plan detailing what he was going to do to hit them.

When we started to hold him accountable in the weekly meetings, he lost it. The CEO was dumbfounded. Squirmy derailed the meetings, and started making excuses for everything, including things that weren't on the agenda. Squirmy re-wrote his own KPIs four times over six weeks, balking at his own work every time.

The CEO finally had to sit down with Squirmy and give him an ultimatum—play by the rules or get off the field. He chose to get off the field.

Cascading KPIs Throughout An Organization

Once you have your strategic KPIs, the next step is to cascade them throughout the organization. The diagram below shows how easy this is to do. As an owner myself, I like to have a third-party coach or consultant walk my team through this graphic, but it's certainly something your team can do on its own.

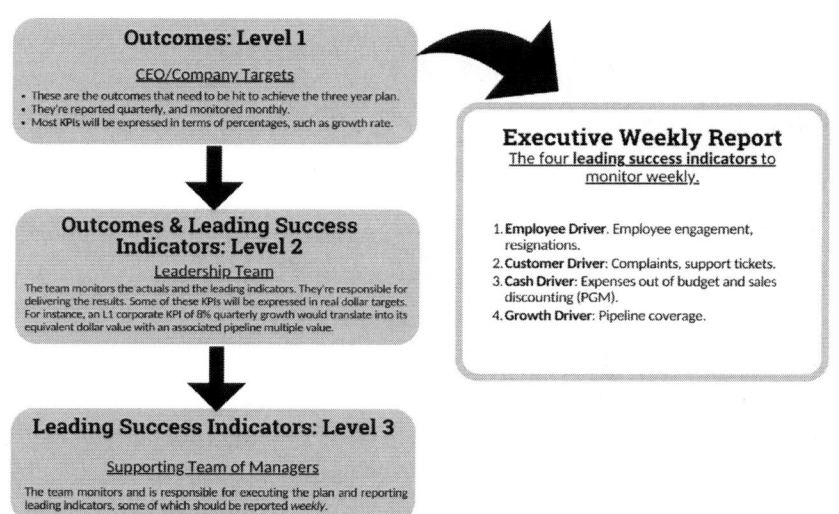

The Catipult Structure
Speed, Clarity and Accountability

Outcomes: Level 1

CEO/Company Targets
- These are the outcomes that need to be hit to achieve the three year plan.
- They're reported quarterly, and monitored monthly.
- Most KPIs will be expressed in terms of percentages, such as growth rate.

Executive Weekly Report
The four **leading success indicators** to monitor weekly.

1. **Employee Driver.** Employee engagement, resignations.
2. **Customer Driver:** Complaints, support tickets.
3. **Cash Driver:** Expenses out of budget and sales discounting (PGM).
4. **Growth Driver:** Pipeline coverage.

Outcomes & Leading Success Indicators: Level 2

Leadership Team
The team monitors the actuals and the leading indicators. They're responsible for delivering the results. Some of these KPIs will be expressed in real dollar targets. For instance, an L1 corporate KPI of 8% quarterly growth would translate into its equivalent dollar value with an associated pipeline multiple value.

Leading Success Indicators: Level 3

Supporting Team of Managers
The team monitors and is responsible for executing the plan and reporting leading indicators, some of which should be reported weekly.

The owners of a business are what we call Level 1 (L1). These L1 KPIs are ones you monitor, and they're also called corporate KPIs. From this level, the second level of KPIs are created as supportive KPIs. If your organization has an executive team, that team monitors the L1 KPIs with you, their own Level 2 (L2) metrics, and those of the team that works for them, Level 3 (L3).

Most small business owners are currently managing at the L2 level. This happens for several reasons. First, if the owner started the company, they began at the base level of metrics...paying bills on time, taking the trash out; you name it, founders do it. Once the company grows, they hire people to work on those basic KPIs and begin to focus on operational issues, Level 2. It's here that most owners stop. While they may hire a team at L2, it doesn't mean the owner shifts their focus away from this level.

The core six KPIs we covered are L1. There are certainly others specific to your company and industry, but not many. I encourage all owners to stay at L1 and let your executives focus on L2.

The Two Triangles For Cascading KPIs

In the L1 Triangle figure, you'll see the core six KPIs we already have covered.

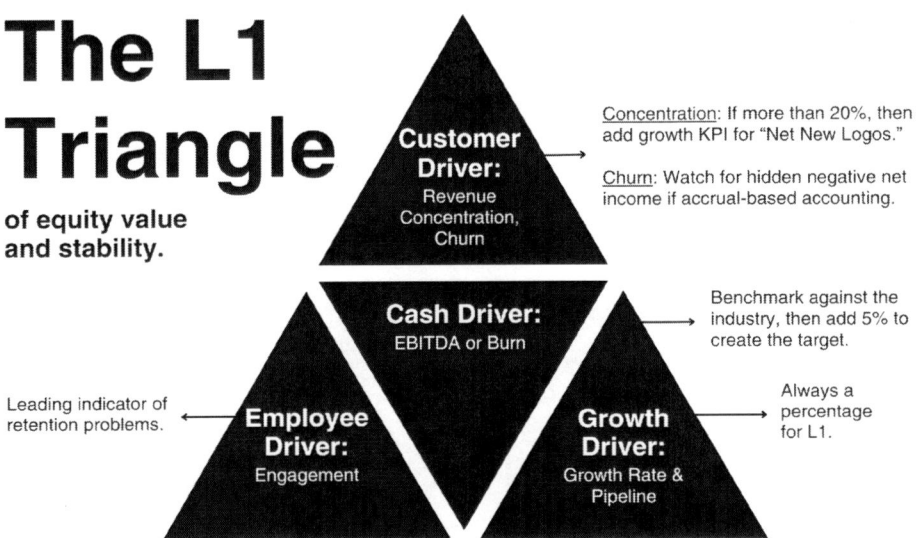

The L2 Triangle gives examples of what your executive team should consider. As you can see, the L2 KPIs clearly support those in L1.

The L2 Triangle of performance to plan.

Customer Driver: Complaints, Support Tickets → Leading indicator of churn.

Cash Driver: Expenses, COGS, PGM → PGM: What products, services have what margins?

Employee Driver: Training %

Growth Driver: Pipeline, Quarterly Revenue, Time to Close → Pipeline: Know the close rate and time to close a deal. Determine the multiple value.

Now, let's use these guides to break down the concentration of revenue. As we know, it needs to be 20 percent or below. Let's say your company is at 35 percent, like the example above. Your team needs to work at reducing the concentration of revenue by 15 percent, and that's associated with your Outcome Statement.

What contributes to a decline in revenue concentration? New customers, not more sales from existing accounts. An L2 KPI for your sales team, therefore, would be: "Net New Customers Per Quarter to Lower Our Concentration of Revenue." Set the target and tell your sales manager to own that KPI.

Here's a chart that further illustrates how to quickly create supporting metrics.

Driver	L1 KPI	L2 KPI
Customer	Churn Rate: 5%	Support Calls/Customer/Year: 2
Customer	Concentration: 20%	Revenue from New Accounts: $5 Million
Cash	EBITDA: 20%	Operational Expenses to Plan: 100%
Growth	Growth Rate: 30%	QX Revenue Target: $1.5 MM
Growth	Pipeline Multiple Two Quarters Ahead of Revenue Target: 3x	Q1 Pipeline for Q2 Revenue: $3 MM
Growth	-	Target Deal Close Time Frame vs Actual
Employee	Engagement Score: 7.4	Employees Trained: 100%

Cheat Sheet

Most of the L1 KPIs won't be monitored weekly. That said, you still need to keep up with the business. To that end, here is a weekly CEO report of L2 KPIs that your team should generate for you weekly. There are only four things, but these four give you all the strategic insight you need into the business.

Executive Weekly Report
The four **leading success indicators** to monitor weekly.

1. **Employee Driver**. Employee engagement, resignations.
2. **Customer Driver**: Complaints, support tickets.
3. **Cash Driver**: Expenses out of budget and sales discounting (PGM).
4. **Growth Driver**: Pipeline coverage.

1. Employee Driver: Monitor your engagement score and resignations.

2. Customer Driver: Monitor complaints and support tickets.

3. Cash Driver: Expenses beyond budget and sales team discounting. Both are sleeper killers of profit.

4. Growth Driver: Pipeline coverage. By having your team report to you every week on pipeline, you'll instill a culture of pipeline development and be able to ward off revenue issues before the quarter ends.

How to Write KPIs

To really accelerate the speed of this system, KPIs need to be written in a concise syntax that makes the metric clear to everyone (a Rockefeller Habit). This syntax is turning your business into numbers and will probably seem awkward at first. Each KPI must have:

Description	Unit of Measurement	Time Period	Target	Actual	Reporting Frequency

Let's break this down by example:

Goal: "We need to reduce our accounts receivable (AR)." This isn't very clear, yet this goal is quite a popular one. The table below illustrates the evolution of a goal into specifics that will become highly actionable and measurable.

Discovery Questions	Client Answer	Your Interpretation
Outcome Statement?	We want our corporate debt paid off.	They want to pay it off and likely have enough operating cash not to use it.
What is the client's definition of "receivable"?	Non-subscription product invoices	Subscription revenue isn't a problem, it is the project-based or product sales that are invoiced.
What does "reduce" mean?	We invoice clients during the project and often, invoices from one phase aren't getting paid until well after the second phase has started.	This scenario could lead to more coaching. However, for KPI-writing's sake, we now know that phased invoicing exists.
Why do they think it's a problem?	We spend our own cash to get the project done and it can cause cash flow issues.	A KPI is needed that syncs with cash balances, AP trends.
What impact is AR having to cash?	We're too cyclical with the revenue.	EMOTION: Stress and anxiety exist
How long has AR been outstanding?	It's been a problem from the start and sometimes we go 45 days into Phase 2 before getting paid on Phase 1.	Lack of clear objects has prevented a clear strategy for AR from being created.
How long do they want it to be outstanding?	Ideally, we'd like Phase 1 to be paid within one week of completion.	One week after Phase 1 ... but when do they invoice?
When do you invoice for Phase 1?	Upon completion, net 7 days	Customers aren't adhering to Net 7. We may have two KPIs coming from this... one for the AR and the second for billing.

Using those answers, both L1 and L2 KPIs can be created.

Possible Ways to Write the KPI	Unit of Measurement	Time Period	Target	Actual	Reporting Frequency
Percent of Project Invoices Paid 7 days after Phase 1 completion	Percentage	Evergreen	95	50	Start out with weekly if this will be a Focus KPI
Average Days Outstanding for Phase 1 Project invoices	Days	Evergreen	7	45	Start out with weekly if this will be a Focus KPI

Strategic L2 KPI	Unit of Measurement	Time Period	Target	Actual	Reporting Frequency
Percent of Phase 1 project invoices sent to customer 30 days before Phase One Completion	Percentage	Evergreen	100	0	Start out with weekly if this will be a Focus KPI

Note: For the L2 KPI, we are making a strategic change to the way they invoice. If the customer invoices Net 30 upon Phase 1 start, the invoice will be queued properly in their client's AP systems.

Look at the clarity that now exists. Rather than simply telling a team to reduce AR, the team now knows that it needs to focus on either increasing the percentage of project invoices paid 7 days after Phase 1 completion from 50 percent to 95 percent and maintain that level continually; or, reducing the average days outstanding for Phase 1 project invoices from 45 days to 7.

While either version works to create tangible supporting actions, the second of the two drives the question, "how?" The L2 KPI answers that question by introducing a new process into the organization to invoice at the beginning of Phase 1, not the end.

When KPIs are taken seriously, they're one of the most important, even most powerful, tools you have as a business owner.

- They allow you to lead instead of manage.

- They allow you to track instead of guess.

- They allow you to plan for success within three years instead of running around hoping for success someday.

- They allow you to say "no" to time wasted in meaningless meetings.

- They allow you to focus on the main thing, and let the main thing be your focus, which is the future, as defined by a twelve-quarter outcome, informed by the data of today.

Data is just a scoreboard. But it isn't about winning or losing. It's about progress.

"Metrics help us understand speed and distance," says Simon Sinek, author of *The Infinite Game*, after noting that if you run a marathon without mile markers, you'll find it disconcerting, because you don't know how far you've progressed.[7]

Industry Expert Interview And Case Studies:
Getting The Scorecard Right

Diane Mentzer

Thanks to Catipult I'm living out an early career dream I had forgotten I had! More about that in a minute. First the serendipitous part: In early 2023, I decided to go out on my own serving as a Fractional COO. Due to competing priorities, getting started took a little longer than planned. And I'm so glad! Because of that, I got introduced to Catipult before I got too far down that road. One of the things that impressed me most was the strategic way Catipult uses AI to get leadership focused on the scorecard right away and create efficiencies for the business owner and leadership team. The other is the freedom coaches have to incorporate inside-the-business advising with on-the-business coaching. It really is the next evolution!

Back to the dream I had when I was working towards my Associate's degree in management: I vividly remember standing in my parents' kitchen telling them that I had figured out my career. I wanted to help companies get set up and running and then come back regularly to check on them and help keep things rolling along. That was a big moment for me!

After earning my bachelor's degree, I entered the real world, started working for an amazing leader at a government contracting firm, and forgot all about that dream.

In 2019, the small business I was working for started self-implementing another operating system and I took on the role of Integrator, as a fraction of my full-time job, and realized that I'd been integrating my whole life. I just never knew it. Being in that role led to my introduction to Catipult.

So now, here I am (I don't want to say how many years later) a Certified Catipult Coach doing exactly what I wanted to do when I was 19, helping businesses get headed in the right direction and providing ongoing monthly support. What's really exciting is that—AI-generated

KPIs and the meeting cadence (which includes a new six-week tactical meeting)—business owners and second in commands see results so much faster than they could have before!

Why is Catipult's ability to provide companies with the six critical KPIs and world-class targets (aka the scorecard) during the onboarding session so remarkable? Because it immediately gets companies on the path to world-class status.

Catipult tells us exactly what every business owner needs to know: here are six KPIs that impact the value of every business, across the board. And here are the world-class targets for those KPIs. This is especially critical because some of these KPIs, like revenue concentration and revenue churn, are things that many business owners have often never thought about or have been measuring incorrectly.

When I was thinking about stories to share, Catipult's pipeline KPI really hit home for me. I knew of a company where the business development director would consistently bring a pipeline to the table that was completely unrealistic. It was the right size, at least three times the target, but the company had no connections to the agencies or opportunities on the pipeline, so they had no shot at winning the work. People pointed out that the pipeline was unrealistic, but the CEO kept that guy around and continued to listen to him, despite no new work coming in. Within a few years, the company went from 220 people to 10-15 people.

There's a measure of realism that needs to take place in pipeline calculations and you need to account for revenue churn and understand how your growth strategy impacts revenue concentration. But the main thing is that it can't just be pie in the sky. You need to know your close rate and timeline and have the ability to bring those deals in: if the close rate is zero percent, then it doesn't matter how fast you think you can close a deal or how big the pipeline is!

As a next generation system, Catipult respects and honors the systems that came before it. While there are complementary aspects,

Catipult is more powerful, launches faster, and is more efficient.

As a fractional Integrator with another business operating system, I could only work with three to four companies at a time. With Catipult, I can help ten! Using very conservative calculations, efficiencies due to reduced email (estimating two hours per week) and shorter meetings, we save the business owner and the members of their leadership team at least 124 hours a year each. Each! Even with the addition of the four-hour six-week tactical meeting. And you know what I think people should do with that time? Something they really love!

On a personal note, Peter's approach of putting the business owner first and incorporating strategies that engage the subconscious to help us succeed are other elements that drew me to Catipult. I've been weaving these kinds of strategies into my leadership and coaching activities for the last few years, so it was validating to see that Catipult is designed on a three-year picture because that's what our brain can handle and the reporting language that helps get around the reticular activating system ("fight or flight mode").

The top three benefits of Catipult, in my opinion, are: 1) how it gets companies up and running so quickly with their scorecard (world-class KPIs with targets); 2) the efficiencies that the system creates and the resulting time savings (124+ hours per year) for everybody using it; and, 3) Certified Catipult Coaches help more business owners and second-in-command get results faster and transform the businesses they run into world-class companies.

Chapter 7: Action Items: Related to KPIs

Have you ever had a day where you ticked fifty boxes off your to-do list, sat back and felt a wave of accomplishment, and then looked at your to-do list one more time only to realize that there were fifty-one new items on the list? Perhaps that wave of accomplishment turned into an undertow, dragging your entire positive mindset out to sea, and you went home discouraged instead of fulfilled.

Or perhaps you were in mid-level management at some point and you were asked to do a report, so you worked for seventy hours on it, only to find out that the data you collected was no longer relevant because the owner had already decided to divest the firm of that division. You turned in your report the day after the division was sold, and your boss said, "Oh, sorry about that. We should have had you doing _____ instead."

Maybe when you were in an entry-level sales position, someone gave you a bunch of things to do that you knew had no bearing on whether you were going to meet your quota, but you did them anyway because if you didn't, you stood to lose your job. The boss said you had to do them, and that was that.

What is wrong with this world and all our frantic action items, rocks, to-dos, or whatever you want to call them? Where did they all come from? How many of them are necessary? Are you managing your performance against the plan? Or are you just performing some sort of high-wire circus act zipping back and forth on a unicycle hoping that your audience (customers, stakeholders, employees, leadership) will say, ooh, aah, and not give a second thought to the fact that you're not getting any closer to your destination?

If these things describe something that has happened to you, I have two things to say. First, do not despair. The world doesn't have to be this way!

Second, if you are in leadership and allow this to continue, you are not only wasting your own time but the time of those you lead as well. Empower people to say, "Boss, what KPI is this related to?" And if you don't have a good answer, then you should reply, "You know what? Forget it. Get back to work on what's important."

One of the things that people love about this system is that no action item or rock can be set if they are not related to a KPI.

Action Item Or Rock?

You may have heard about the idea of the "rock". The rock is a metaphor for the heavy thing that needs to be done and lifted into a hole, but often doesn't get moved because it is heavy and takes too long. Instead, the tendency owners and teams have is spending their time filling the gap with sand (going about the daily grind) because it is much easier to move, even though it takes a lot more sand to fill the gap that one big rock could easily do.

The rock is a great metaphor and strategy that has helped many owners succeed at getting one or two big projects done in a quarter.

In business reality, however, it leaves much to be desired. While it's nice to try to believe that only one or two major things should be done in the quarter, we often find ourselves with several projects that are strategic and must happen sooner than the quarter's end. Those systems don't have a place for *whatever that is*, so teams tend to place them on a spreadsheet outside the system they're using. There they sit...not directly attached to a strategy or one of the big projects, but they certainly aren't sand, either.

It's this dysfunction that led my clients and me to create the idea of an *action item* and made sure it was part of the Catipult user interface. Action items are projects or initiatives that must be done within a quarter or by the end of a quarter. By contrast, rocks are very rigid in their definition. They are the only things that are due at the end of each quarter.

Action items are flexible enough and can even be recurring. For instance, you may want to make sure that your marketing VP reviews market conditions annually on the same date every year. Market analysis is no small task and can take months. To make sure this happens, we designed our system so that recurring action items can be created. For example, you may need your assistant to prepare quarterly reports. This may take time and would make a great recurring action item.

Action items are not tasks. Tasks are things that support an action item's completion. Each task is listed under an action item, which is, in turn, attached to a KPI and business driver.

Let's Show How That All Works

First, I'm serious about this: *Every single* action item must be attached to an existing reason for that action item. That reason, of course, is your KPI. So that's the way the Catipult system works, because you're going to create a purpose-driven organization. If someone is doing a survey... to them, it's easy to get the impression, *I'm just doing a survey. What does it matter?*

But when that survey is attached directly to something like a Net Promoter Score (NPS), you can ask them, "What are you working on today?"

Instead of saying, "Some boring survey I have to do," they can say, "Hey, I'm working on creating the best NPS possible; we're working toward an 80 percent, which is a KPI in the Customer Driver."

"Well, how are you doing that?"

"Well, today I'm working on a survey so we can measure that."

In this way, every leader in your organization—and every employee, too—begins to realize their *action item* is where the rubber meets the road. And that's the way to get you and your entire organization working towards that three-year outcome every single day. When you're thinking about those action items, and you're putting them into the Catipult system, don't use it as a to-do list!

Ideas for *action items* can come from every quarter. You're going to get lots of ideas from lots of different people, even (maybe especially) yourself. You'll always have those big-idea people around, and they're always saying:

"Hey, we ought to do such and so, that would be great!"

But if that idea cannot attach to a KPI, then you need to ask the question, "Is it really something we should be working on?" In many cases, the answer is no.

When you're creating an action item, it has to be associated with a KPI. That's why there's no way around it in our system. By this, we show everyone: *This is how I'm going to impact what it is I need to accomplish.* It's really easy for your team to use.

Recurring Action Items

Your action items can actually be things that recur on a weekly, monthly, or quarterly basis. Perhaps it's a quarterly report. Maybe it's a weekly safety check. If it's in an employee's job description (or needs to be added to their job description) and you want to make sure that they are checking up on it, all you have to do is make the *action item* a recurring one.

Speed In Planning

Minds work better and faster when clear guide rails for thought are presented. Doctors, for instance, don't use unstructured formats to diagnose patients. The military has rigid processes for just about every area of decision making. World-class companies are no different. The more objective you can make the decision-making process, the faster solutions can be found, while increasing the likelihood of success when the decisions are made.

The two key words are *faster and successful*. Doctors need to decide quickly and their diagnosis must be correct. The military needs to act quickly and in a way that ensures safety for all the troops. That's why both the military and medical fields have developed written protocols to reduce feelings-based decisions and enhance objectivity.

The Seven Business Drivers Adds Speed to Problem Solving

This structure helps you do the same in your business.

Look through the Seven Business Drivers™. They are your new context for thinking quickly about the business. What metrics are needed for each of the drivers? How is the leadership team faring? What is the retention rate of the employees we want to keep? You get the idea. By using this logic tree, you're able to move more quickly through the business.

In the figure, you can see how this works. Look at each driver and then the example KPIs attached to them. The business is being translated into numbers and strategic, measurable objectives that must be achieved for you to meet the desired outcome.

You're also seeing yourself and your own personal goals in-line with those of the business for the first time. This is a powerful visual not only for you, but also your employees. In fact, one CEO mentioned that the "You" driver was the number one catalyst for down-stream adoption of Catipult in her company. Her employees loved it.

Without having to say a word, she was demonstrating to them that she created a culture where personal goals and well-being were valued and to be measured equally with those of business.

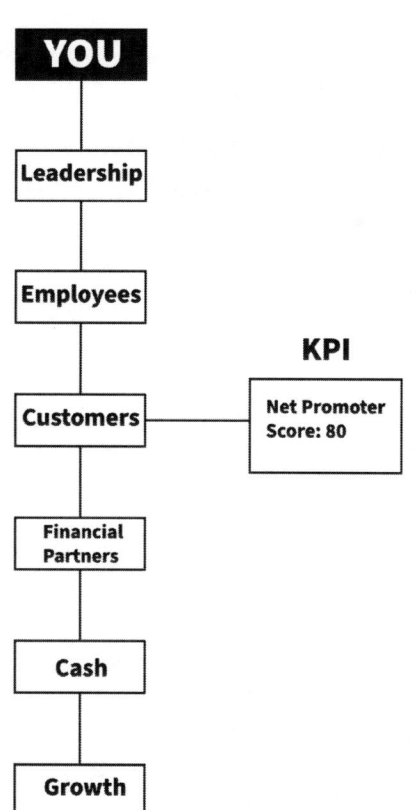

In the Catipult software, the You Driver KPIs are completely private. While employees did choose to share some of their personal goals with their managers, it was their choice to make. Among the goals shared with her, she said, were sobriety stages, weight-loss, time with the family, books to read, and additional professional development courses.

When using this with your management team, meetings are streamlined as they now have what many meetings lack—focus. Give the brain a problem to solve, and it will solve it. Give the brain ambiguity and it will wonder for hours in search of a clear problem. You may have experienced this "wondering" in your meetings.

Before implementing this

system, I worked with a team that seemed to enjoy meandering around issues. If it was an 8-hour meeting, you could count on them to not define the clear problem until the six-hour mark. When this system was presented to them, their meeting time was cut in half without any pressure, without rushing them. Their brains just worked much more quickly.

Action Items With A Purpose

In the figure, the logic continues to expand. Now, we're creating action items attached to specific KPIs. As touched upon in the previous chapter that discussed the Seven Business Drivers, a purpose-driven company is created instantly with this system.

The support ticket KPI may be a static KPI for years. The action items to keep that KPI at target may change monthly or quarterly.

Let's Unpack This

Picture yourself in a quarterly meeting. Your team is there. Rather than pulling up slideware, you pull up the corporate KPIs you selected as areas of focus for this meeting. One of those KPIs is the one on the following page, two support tickets per year per customer. The actual performance is three. The team just needs to reduce the number of tickets by 1 per customer.

You: "Team, the first thing we're going to cover is the support ticket KPI. We're close. Good work. I want each department to take 15 minutes to come up with two things it believes it can do to help get this number to two by the end of the next quarter. We'll discuss the ideas, choose which to implement, and move onto to the next focus KPI for today."

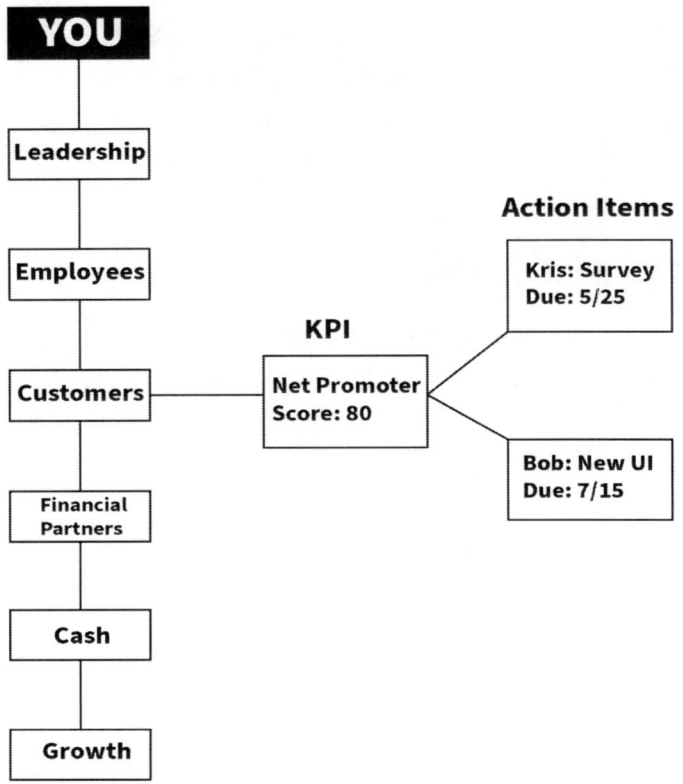

Fifteen minutes later, you have two action items or projects for each department. After agreeing on them, each department head adds their action items underneath the same KPI. Now, you and the team can quickly see how each department is contributing to this objective. After the meeting, teams can add the tasks they need to get done to make sure their chosen action item is completed on time.

You move on to the next focus KPI.

Clarity And Attachment To The Bigger Picture

Proverbs 29:18 says, "Without a vision, people perish." This could easily happen to Kris and Bob, responsible for the action items (brochure and survey) in the figure. Without this system, the work they do is not attached to any vision or overall goal and occurs as just another task. With the direct attachment to the corporate goal, they are now strategic collaborators with you and your vision.

How much more energy would you have in your company if every employee felt like a strategic collaborator with you, rather than just a "doer of projects?" As you begin to hire Generation Z, you'll want to make sure that you read them into the vision and purpose. This new generation of extremely bright people want—and almost demand—to be in the loop. This gets them there while maintaining structural continuity.

Action Items: When KPIs Aren't Yet Clear

Sometimes, when I'm getting things set up with a client and they're unclear on a KPI, the first action item related to that KPI is to get the initial numbers for the KPI. For example, a company doesn't know what their pipeline is. Someone probably has a vague idea of how many bids they've done in the past three months and how much volume has been quoted in those bids, and someone else probably has an idea of the average amount of time it takes to close and the percentage of bids that are won, but nobody has anything precise yet. The problem is, you can't solve a delta if you don't know both the target you want to hit and a precise starting point. What's your pipeline today? So that becomes the first action item related to the KPI: get definition on the KPI itself. What are the numbers?

In fact, it may be easier to come up with the numbers you want to see in your outcome statement than to find the numbers that correspond to that number in today's terms, in today's data, since your outcome statement is being developed in your imagination.

Another example of this would be in the Growth Driver. You would think owners and leaders would know what their current revenue is, but I've talked with people whose businesses are so complex they don't even have that basic statistic at their fingertips. *How much revenue have we made, year-to-date? Do we want to use numbers starting from the end of the previous quarter, or previous year? Or do we want to start with...?* Rather than get into a lengthy discussion while setting up a new KPI, you can set up a placeholder in that KPI and assign someone the action item of making sure you've got a good handle on your starting point, getting definition. How can you go from A to B if you've defined B, but you don't know where A is?

Assigning Action Items

Catipult makes it easy to assign an action item to someone in the leadership level (what we call L2), or even a level below your executive team (L3 to L10).

As a business owner you may be used to crunching the numbers yourself, in the wee hours of the night, either for fun or out of anxiety and worry. But again, I'm not interested in seeing business owners have to do everything. Delegation is the name of the game. Whether it's a bookkeeper or CFO, someone else can find the metrics, solve the deltas, and do almost everything that needs to be done. So don't do it yourself. Assign that action item and make sure you know exactly when it needs to be done. Once you've delegated something, you ought to have a system in place that will remind you later, so you don't have to devote valuable grey matter cells to remembering when the action item should be reported on. If you have to do that, you might as well do the deed yourself. Know that it will be coming back up in a few weeks, and that your employee can see it on their dashboard. Then forget about it until your system tells you it is time to get that report. Delegation isn't really delegation if you're still worrying about it.

Deadlines: Artificial And Arbitrary, Or Hard And Fast?

Think about the last time you put something off until it was no longer relevant. You decided not to do it by delaying it until it didn't matter anymore. Perhaps it was a task at a job you left when someone else hired you. Perhaps it was as simple as not mowing the lawn one last time in the fall, and then, when winter set in and snow covered your grass.

Action items mean nothing without deadlines. Some items are recurring, others are one-time only, but there are two kinds of deadlines. The first is what we could call arbitrary and artificial.

An entrepreneur recently told me, "I need to make a decision about which path to pursue with my life by the end of the month; will I build business A next, or put my focus on business B?" After further discussion, I realized that in this case, the entrepreneur had nobody else who needed this decision by that date. There were no partners involved, and there was nothing that was out of his own control, no data or information or relational confirmation that he had to wait for. The decision was his to make at any time he wanted to make it. I said, "If you're going to create artificial and arbitrary deadlines for yourself, then I have to challenge you to follow through and make the decision on that day."

Why would I say that? Because the more we set artificial and arbitrary deadlines for ourselves and *don't follow through*, the less we believe in ourselves. That's a recipe for getting stuck in quicksand of your own design. I had to challenge him to take himself seriously when it came to his own self-imposed deadline. I knew he was already frustrated, postponing decisions about such things would only increase his discouragement.

This is another reason why three-year outcomes are so important. You give your brain an opportunity to rise to the occasion and accept the challenge of getting to a certain place by a certain time.

The alternative deadline is what I would call *hard and fast*. It's much less negotiable. April 15th is Tax Day in the United States, and while you can technically file extensions, and you may even have good reason to do so from time to time, the basic reality is that those unfiled documents or extensions may bring unneeded additional stress. We could say that the deadline for filing taxes is not in your control, it is mandated by the government. It is not yours to decide. It is a hard and fast deadline.

Be clear with yourself and with your team when setting deadlines for action items and be clear with those you lead, as well. If you allow your direct reports to delay deadlines you've indicated are hard and fast, they'll only begin to believe that you meant they were artificial and arbitrary.

On the other hand, if they truly are artificial and arbitrary, it might be better to say, "I'd like to have a report by Monday, but the real deadline is April 15."

Be honest about which kind of deadline you're setting, and you'll breed clarity for yourself and others.

CHAPTER 8: FASTER MEETINGS, BETTER RESULTS

I'll just come out and admit it: I hate meetings.

That might seem strange when you realize that during the years I've been coaching, the primary thing I do is *meet* with my clients.

We'll discuss how to find a good coach later, but here's one tip about a good coach: a good coach shouldn't sell based on how much of their own time they're going to give you. They sell you based on how much of *your own time* they're going to save you over the long term!

Imagine having a meeting with a coach that's booked for an hour. After thirty minutes you've discussed everything you need to discuss so that you can move forward with the next part of your plan. You've had some sort of epiphany, a reframing of your problem, or a great discussion about strategy. You even came away with a few new tactics to try in the next week. Then, your coach asks, "Anything else you'd like to discuss?" And you say "no, not today."

"Great. I'll see you next time," says the coach, and that's the end of the discussion. That's a marker for a good, if not an excellent, coach. They just gave you 30 minutes back.

I've seen rookie coaches at work and believe me when I tell you this: rookie coaches take longer to get you there. Longer meetings do not always equate to increased productivity. Having a meeting about getting a cover designed for this book with my graphic designer may be necessary if the designer will be able to proceed in a productive manner, but a meeting is not the same as spending time writing the book, nor is it the same as the designer spending time designing the book cover.

Meetings aren't programming new software, shooting a commercial, troubleshooting a problem for a customer; meetings aren't really anything but a bridge. But at the same time, meetings are often termed "productive" or "unproductive." Like a bridge, they either get you across the chasm or they don't.

One of the best indicators that a meeting was productive is to look at how short it was. If everyone walks away from the meeting in alignment, knowing what to do next, what does it matter if it only took thirty seconds?

Frank, a manager on a shop floor, approaches a blue-collar fellow running a machine. Bobby isn't a chatty guy, but he can really crank out some parts. Bobby loves working on piece rate, and he doesn't really like it when Frank interrupts him!

"Hey, Bobby," Frank says, "Joe from Acme Corp. called. He wants the parts for project B tomorrow and said that project A can wait."

Bobby nods. He moves a cart of parts away from his machine (parts for project A) and pulls parts for project B to his workstation. In a minute, he's changed the programming to calibrate the machine for project B and has his machine humming away. In an hour, the parts are on the loading dock. They will be delivered to Joe at Acme Corp. first thing in the morning.

The meeting took ten seconds. Two people were involved. One said nothing.

Why should boardroom meetings take any longer? Put a team in place who understands what they're doing so well they can simplify things for non-experts (and that starts with you, too: your CFO most likely understands finance better than you do). Expect people to communicate clearly and get the heck out of there.

Elon Musk has six rules[8] to minimize length of meetings, which requires communicating clearly, but perhaps has more to do with developing a culture for meetings. Get away from large meetings unless you're sure you're adding value. Reduce meeting frequency, as well.

"Musk recommends that people 'walk out of a meeting or drop off a call as soon as it is obvious you aren't adding value. It is not rude to leave, it is rude to make someone stay and waste their time.'"

Musk's other rules are focused on common sense and communicating clearly, and that's where the Catipult.AI CHARP check-in system comes into play.

CHARP – More information About The Status Of A Project, Instantly

CHARP is a check-in system I developed with the assistance of twenty business owners and their executive teams. It's fast, accurate, and culturally transformative. CHARP allows team members to designate a certain status to any project, action item, or process. It is designed to not only allow for clear communication, but communication that is blame-free. This will help you build a culture that avoids superfluous micro-management. It allows people to ask for help without shame or fear of judgment. Building a culture that allows everyone to report a status in a non-judgmental environment is one way to move things forward smoothly without anyone hiding, playing games, or using corporate speak to dodge responsibility.

The check-in system was born through a tragic experience. In my group meetings, we would begin each meeting by checking on personal, business, health and a few other things using a scale of 1-10. Lower numbers were not good; higher were better.

One morning, I received a call from Bill. He told me he wasn't coming to the group because his wife had left him. I refused to let him miss and drove to his house to give him a ride. He came to the group, intending to tell them what had happened, and he gave me permission to help him break the news to the group.

We started the meeting with our routine check-in. Everyone checked in on a scale of 1 to 10. Everyone scored themselves between 8 and 10, including Bill! Granted, some may consider a motion to vacate by a spouse a great thing, but I knew Bill was devastated.

I called an audible. It wasn't just Bill who fudged his check-in, I knew of others who had aspects of their lives below a five. We stopped the meeting in its tracks. Bill confessed that his life was really a 1 out of 10 right now, which led the rest of the owners to sheepishly admit they weren't really giving honest answers, either.

We then had a fantastic and very powerful group discussion. The 1-10 system, they said, was judgmental. No one wanted to be perceived the "loser in life." That day, we abandoned the 1-10 check-in system and built CHARP. Many Vistage groups now use it for their check-ins and the owners who helped develop it with me use it in their companies. We had posters made and everything.

CHARP uses non-judgmental words with very specific definitions *and* action items attached to each one. It gives you immediate, actionable information on the status of an action item. Just scan all the action items and their status and you'll know in seconds what is going on in your company.

CHARP is:
- Change
- Help
- Aware
- Redirect
- Plan

Let's go in depth on each of the five.

Change: Something beyond your control has happened in the middle of the process and may cause a delay, affecting your ability to complete the milestone as planned or on time. As John Lennon famously said, "Life is what happens when you're making other plans." No matter how bulletproof you thought your plan was, life is going to throw change at you every day. Change can come from supply chain issues, employee health issues, accidents, flood, or fire. When someone marks something they're responsible for as "Change" it doesn't necessarily mean the person needs help.

Help: This is a way for a team member to indicate that they need help. There's no shame in needing help; none of us are getting where we're going on our twelve-month outcomes without helping one another. In many companies, people feel a request for help may not be well received. The CHARP system makes Help an integral part of life on the job. It's one of five statuses you can choose, it's baked into the system. When you need help or advice from others, ask for it. You may be depending on a vendor or another department for advice or need their cooperation. When you choose to mark something "Help" you're just letting people know that without assistance, your milestone is in jeopardy.

Aware: An event has occurred that may cause a delay or adjustment to the plan. When you use the "Aware" designation, this means that despite changes happening around you, you have a milestone under control, believing you are likely to hit the milestone. You are aware that there may be a situation that could impact the deliverable, so you're letting people know you're aware. When an action item is marked "Aware" the person who is responsible for seeing it through is letting your executive team know that they may want to make you aware of something, but they may have *no need for help.* More on awareness in the section about Discussions.

Redirect: This designation is like "Change," but Redirect is about change that's under your control. You feel the situation warrants a change to the plan. An example of a redirect would be when you feel it is in the best interest of the company to either accelerate or decelerate a certain project: you find a bug in the software that could harm someone, and it's going to take time to fix. Or you learn that a competitor is releasing their software early and yours is ready to go, so you feel it would be best to accelerate your release date as well.

"Redirect" is a great way for the people you lead to offer suggestions based on their own expertise in the process. This is a way to let everyone know, "I learned something about the business environment you should know, so that we can consider a different approach."

Plan: In an organization that's humming along with everyone playing their roles, taking responsibility for their work, asking for help when they need it, and paying attention to changes so that they're aware of any possible hiccups, most action items and projects are on plan. Projects which are marked as on Plan *do not require discussion in a meeting! This alone will save you many hours per week!*

C	H	A	R	P
Change	Help	Aware	Redirect	Plan
A change happened beyond your control that is impacting your plan.	You are not hitting some of your milestones.	An event is occurring that may cause delay or cause an adjustment to your plan.	You are choosing to redirect your plan based on new information or events.	You are on plan.
Action:	Action:	Action:	Action:	Action:
Monitor, research and adjust.	Let the team know that help is required for you to hit your objective or deadline.	Quickly tell the team what is happening and how you are working through the situation.	Change elements of your strategic plan. Communicate your intention with your colleagues.	Don't view this as good or bad. It just is. Monitor conditions to make sure your plan is what it should be.

Changing Our Language

©Copyright, Catpult, Inc
https://www.catipult.ai

Consider the example above where Joe from Acme Corp. needed *Help*: he needed parts for Project B delivered before parts for Project A. He called his supplier, Frank, and requested help. Frank went to talk to Bobby; Frank offered a *redirect*: the client requested a different product delivered first; it was now to everyone's advantage to delay one project and finish another instead. As soon as Bobby became *aware*, as he indicated by a simple nod of the head, he switched from one project (Project A) to another, (Project B) and might have marked *"Change"* on Project A. You may think you're running something more complicated than a machine shop... but chances are, when it comes to CHARP, it isn't. Like the six KPIs we discussed in Chapter 3, the five statuses of CHARP should work in just about every business setting.

Heck, these five items could even work magic in your home life!

Imagine the following scenario: A wife calls her husband and says, "I need **Help**: Our daughter has to get to a dentist appointment at 4 and we are on the way there now, but the school called and said that Melissa had a fender bender. I happened to know she was going to bring snacks for the soccer team at six, and I told them we would handle it. I know it's a **Change**, but could you please pick up snacks for the soccer team on your way to the game?" At this point, the husband recognizes that his spouse is the CEO of the household, and she has made an executive decision. He could grumble that she's volunteered him, but what good would that do? She has already made the commitment and is asking for help. Now, it's time to get on board with the new **Plan**.

So, he says, "Thanks for making me **Aware**. I was going to mow the lawn this evening, but I'll **Redirect** that and go to the store for snacks instead."

His organized wife says, "Great. We're back on **Plan**. See you at the soccer game, babe."

Yes, to be fair and inclusive, this could be a husband redirecting his C-Suite wife on the family social calendar, too. Either way, imagine how using CHARP language could help your communication in your home life. If it works at work, it'll work at home. And if it works at home, it can change your life for the better.

Catipult Software Tip

When you get to a meeting and see that everyone has their action items marked as either On Plan or Aware, the meeting is over. The only things that need to be discussed are changes, redirections, and requests for help. And if any of those things can be discussed in a sidebar meeting, where only those to whom the discussions pertain are present, you can plan those meetings and conclude the current one.

This is the beauty of the Catipult.AI dashboard: of course, our dashboard also allows someone to mark an action as "Done," which removes the item from the action item list, unless it is a recurring item, such as "send the CEO a monthly report on Employee Engagement," in which case it will show up again at the appropriate due date.

Now that we've covered the basic language that we've used in building a non-judgmental meeting culture, we'll discuss the nuts and bolts of how to run a meeting.

World-Class Meeting Rhythm

Now that we have the check-in process adding speed, we can slide into the rhythm that makes the entire process move your company more quickly. The meeting agendas you'll experience below all work on the KPI model we discussed and are twice as fast as you are likely experiencing now. My goal is to help you keep up or even improve upon the trend toward maximum productivity—getting as much done as possible in as little time as possible.

There's a trend toward speed: Business owners are gravitating to gyms like F45® and Orange Theory® because they can get more for bang for their buck – the "buck" in this equation represents not the almighty dollar, but the almighty *minute.*

Books, too, are getting shorter; authors are focusing more on what needs to be said and saying it in a memorable way, and then getting on with things. If an average business book in the 1980s was 350 pages, the average now is half that, and shrinking.

You only need to do a few things in a meeting: reinforce the KPIs that need to be achieved and monitored, hold members accountable for achieving the items determined as necessary for achieving those KPIs, and allow adequate but not too much time for processing issues, particularly for those items marked as *Change, Help* and *Redirect.*

Why not too much time? Because if you give everyone extra time, people will find a way to fill the time talking about the Baltimore Ravens® or their favorite crypto flavor of the month.

Catipult's "Weekly 80"

The 80-minute weekly meeting is a critical step to kicking off a successfully aligned week for your leadership team. The purpose of your weekly meeting is to keep people informed, hold them accountable and identify any concerns or issues that need resolution. During your meeting, you will be identifying issues along the way that will be discussed and likely resolved.

Eighty minutes is a very intentional amount of time. On the one hand, it adds the necessary pressure required for people to speak efficiently, while on the other hand, it avoids artificially capping discussions early. It also has a logical 10-minute buffer, as most subsequent meetings any person may have during the day will not start for 10 minutes after the Weekly 80 has ended. (For example: the Weekly 80 ends at 8.20 a.m., everyone's next meeting begins at 8.30.) This reduces the stress of hurrying into another back-to-back meeting and gives people 10 minutes to get to their next meeting or delegate new items to their team members that may have arisen during the weekly meeting.

Don't be surprised if the Weekly 80 gets done in 40 minutes or less. Many clients have told me that once they become comfortable with the process, the time spent weekly was cut in half.

Running Your Meeting

Before the meeting: The meeting will not be productive if attendees do not update their KPIs, action items, and issues before attending the meeting. Treat this seriously. Updating four to eight KPIs and Action Items, whether it is done on a shared spreadsheet or in the Catipult.AI system, shouldn't take more than a few minutes. Everyone should add notes for anything that is not on "Plan."

Principle: Running a meeting on bad or lacking data wastes 80 minutes.

Here is the agenda for the Weekly 80.

Meeting Flow

1. You Driver personal goal update, 1 minute each.

2. Review focus KPIs marked in red, 2 minutes per person. Note issues for later.

3. Review rocks/action items marked in red, 2 minutes per person. Note issues for later.

4. Meeting facilitator or owner/CEO prioritizes the most important issues for discussion and leads a discussion on each in order of priority. If an issue requires only 2 people to discuss it, the facilitator may ask them to create a sidebar meeting rather than discussing it in the presence of people who don't need to be there.

5. Score the meeting.

6. Members should add any new action items to their dashboard immediately following the meeting.

Let's go in depth on each one of these five items for the meeting flow:

1. The YOU Driver (Personal)

Start every meeting with a quick overview of how attendees are doing on at least one personal goal. Keep it quick—1 minute per person. A good facilitator will be positive and affirming in an authentic way.

2. Review KPIs

We've already discussed how as the business owner you have six KPIs to track (plus personal KPIs). First, make sure that you have no more than 4 KPIs that need to be reviewed each week for each team member. You will have two minutes to review their four KPIs. This is essentially equivalent to a scorecard. (In the Catipult system, you can even choose which KPIs are worthy of appearing in any meeting by turning on the "Focus" button in the KPI modal.)

How to review KPIs

Skip all KPIs that are on target (green).

Review each team members' KPIs that are not on target (red). Do they need to be discussed? Sometimes the answer is yes; other times, it might be okay to skip them. If a red KPI needs to be discussed, *don't start discussing it right away!* Instead, add it to the discussions list and frame the problem in the notes like this: "The target is 10 and we are accomplishing 8, we need to solve for 2." Do not spend too much time on the review. While a team member is going through their review, additional issues may be identified. Those should be added to the issues list and not discussed until all members have finished their check-in.

The leader should choose the issues that need resolution immediately and be careful not to force a linear progression through the issues. Not all issues carry the same weight or urgency; not all issues need to be discussed by the entire group, either.

3. How to Review the Rocks/Action Items (2 minutes per person)

Every action item must be attached to a KPI. Here is how to review the action items: Make sure the team updates their action items prior to the meeting and adds notes to each action item that is not on Plan. Skip all action items that have been checked in as "on Plan" or "Aware".

Cover all action items with a Help (H) designation. Ask what help they need. If it ends up being something that needs discussion, then add it to the issues list. If it is relatively simple, then field the request and put the results in the notes section of the Action Item.

For items with a Change (C) or Redirect (R) designation, have the team member *briefly* discuss what happened, but do not allow the group to spend time discussing the Change or Redirect at length unless an issue arises that warrants high priority.

4. How to Review Issues

By the time you have reviewed all the items in red, (Help, Change, and Redirect) you will have effectively identified issues throughout the meeting as well as any items that were added before the meeting by team members. Now it is time to discuss and solve the issues.

This phase can either make or break a meeting. So far, things have gone quickly and smoothly. Now team members have an opportunity to discuss issues in more depth. Here are some tips to keep the meeting productive and avoid rabbit trails.

- Assign someone to monitor a timer. Often, people can get into a discussion and miss the timer.

- Make sure that everyone knows the purpose is to solve the issue, not just randomly discuss it.

- A best practice is to not move on to the next issue until a solution is created. That solution could be to do further research, which means action items must be created – don't forget to connect them to a KPI.

Store all issue notes in the "Issue" itself. This keeps the notes for the issue owner to reference after the meeting.

Whether you use Catipult or another reporting system, capture the data while you're in the moment!

5. Ending & Scoring the Meeting

What worked well, and what didn't?

Meetings are creepy, organic creatures from the black lagoon, and they, like any monster, must be kept in check. Ask each person to score the meeting on a scale of 1-10. Consider things like whether it concluded on time, whether they felt heard, and whether they felt the issues discussed were indeed well prioritized by the facilitator. If the average score is 8/10 or better, you're in good shape. If not, ask each person to note what could be improved.

For those who've elected to try Catipult, you'll note that when the meeting is ready to end, the Catipult software will force the team to collectively score the meeting. Here is how to do it:

- Ask one member to be the "math person." They are going to find the average score given by meeting attendees.

- Ask everyone to score the meeting from 1 – 10. The "math person" tracks the score and then reveals the average.

- The average is then added to Catipult when the meeting concludes and scoring notes from members are placed in the scoring record.

For any average below an eight the system will require notes to be added. Notes should focus only on suggestions to improve the next meeting.

Conclusion

Effective meetings take work and dedication. Follow this process. Trust it. It will deliver results.

The Six-Week Tactical Meeting

Now that we have covered the Weekly 80, you're ready to rock and roll. And what is rock? Guitars, a singer, and bass or keyboards, sure, but when it comes to rhythm, rock is all about the backbeat, or an emphasis on the second and fourth beat in a measure. Six weeks into a quarter is similar; it's like the second beat of a measure, it's where you find the groove. Rhythm is all about staying on top of your three-year outcome statements. But the six-week tactical meeting, in the middle of the quarter, isn't about making new outcome statements or strategizing at all. This six-week tactical meeting is the driving force behind the rhythm, because without it, you could easily be out of step by the end of the quarter. DO NOT skip this meeting.

Brain science, experience, and testimonials from clients all suggest that a 12-week space between meetings is too long of a gap and does not afford the opportunity for the tight accountability a company needs to be world-class. Additionally, the absence of a tactical meeting can deprive either a third-party coach or an in-house facilitator of especially important operational information about what the team is getting done and how they're doing it.

What Is A Tactical Meeting?

A tactical meeting is a four-hour space held mid-quarter to review the objectives due at the end of the quarter, discuss their progress, remove any blockers to getting those projects done, and to help the team move forward toward their end-of-quarter goals.

What The Tactical Meeting Is NOT

The tactical meeting is not a strategic meeting. There is nothing strategic about it and the coach or facilitator's job is to make sure it stays that way. Getting bogged down in strategic discussions beyond what needs to be completed in the remaining weeks of the quarter will risk prolonging the meeting beyond four hours and risk making the meeting unproductive. You, as the business owner and big-picture-thinker, may be tempted to discuss future strategies, but keep in mind that the job here is to do what's needed for tactical purposes and get out. Any deviation from the tactical will jeopardize the purpose and the value you want to get from this meeting.

In-Person Meeting Room Setting

Setting up the room is important, and it should be set up differently than the room you will use for a strategic meeting.

1. Bring the CHARP Poster.

2. Bring the 7 Business Drivers Poster.

3. Print the Mission, Vision, Values, and Outcome Statement of the company as well as the KPIs, Action Items, and Issues to discuss. (If using Catipult, you can print the board report in one minute and hey presto you are ready for the meeting.)

4. Bring pens and notepads.

Attire For An In-Person Meeting

It is hard to require certain attire to be worn for any meetings, but if you have a team that is willing and able to play along, then suggest that the team comes in comfortable clothes; the kind they would wear at home on a Saturday.

Why? Psychologically, attire does set a mood. This is a working meeting, not a strategic one, and we want people's minds set appropriately before they even enter the room.

Meeting Pre-Work

There is no meeting pre-work beyond the normal updates the team is required to do before each of their weekly meetings. By the time you get to your first Six-Week Tactical, you should have that part down.

NOTE: The meeting will not be productive if attendees do not update their KPIs, action items, and issues before the meeting. Treat this seriously. Updating takes just five minutes. Running a meeting on bad or lacking data wastes three hours.

1. Have each person update their action items using the CHARP method.

2. For all action items that are not checked-in on Plan, have them add notes directly to the action item in the Action Item.

3. If they have issues to discuss that are not related to an action item in their plan, have them create an issue in your system. (In the Catipult system they can easily send it to this tactical meeting by choosing it from the drop-down menu in the issues pop-up.)

Meeting Pre-Work For The Facilitator Or Coach

1. To keep this meeting running at speed, review your plans and make sure to focus only on the KPIs that have action items *with due dates in the quarter.*

2. Make sure the appropriate team members are invited to the Six-Week Tactical.

3. **Bring a timer!**

Running Your Six-Week Tactical Meeting

1. You Driver Check-in – 10 minutes

Start every meeting with a quick overview of how attendees are doing on at least one personal goal. Keep it quick—the maximum time allowed is only 10 minutes, regardless of the size of the management team.

2. Review the Mission, Vision, and Values – 5 minutes

Choose three volunteers to read aloud the mission, vision, and value statements.

3. Review the Focus Areas – 10 minutes

First, make sure that you have those focus KPIs highlighted for each team member. This is equivalent to a scorecard. Only have the KPIs with Action Items due by the quarter's end visible (in the Catipult system, you can toggle items as in Focus or not). Have each team member validate the KPI actual vs target by going around the room. You will not spend much time reviewing the KPIs because this meeting is not going to focus on solving the "delta" between the target and the actual, but *rather on the Action Items* attached to each KPI.

4. Review the Status of the Major Projects Due for Completion This Quarter – 20 minutes

Here is how to review the Action Items for this meeting:

Skip all Action Items with a status of "P." Do not spend time on these; they are on plan. (Do verify that the status of each Action Item is correct, as even though preparation for the meeting required each person to update their status, realistically, we know that some team members may not have updated their data prior to the meeting.)

Make sure you do not let the team start discussing the projects, until you have gone around to each person present at the meeting to review their statuses!

5. Discuss and Solve Focus Areas and Projects – 120 minutes

In this section, you will spend time facilitating a focused discussion on the projects that are in progress and any issues related to them or the new issues that the team may have added to the issues list.

NOTE: *While a bio-break is not listed in the agenda, make sure you plan one halfway through this section.*

Step 1: Prioritize

- Cover all action items with a Help (H) designation. Take a look at the notes the team member added to the specific action item. Ask them to describe the situation and what help they need. If it ends up being something that needs further discussion, then add it to the issues list.

- For items with a Change (C) or Redirect (R) designation, have the team member discuss what happened, but do not spend time discussing it further unless an issue arises.

- Prioritize the H, C, and Rs by order of complexity, urgency, and impact on the quarter. Score each item on a scale of 1-10 based on this system.

  - Complexity: How much discussion time does this issue take to resolve?

  - Urgency: Do we need to solve it in this meeting?

  - Impact: What level of impact does it have on hitting our quarterly objectives?

Scoring (1 – 10 scale, one is low; ten is high)

	Action Item 1	Action Item 2
Complexity	1	5
Urgency	9	4
Impact	3	10
SCORE	13	19

This scoring model creates an objective view of each issue and helps the team collectively understand which issues must be resolved in this meeting.

NOTE: *Keep the pace moving. Do not get bogged down in discussions.*

Step 2: Facilitate

At this point, the coach or facilitator needs to use their discretion on how best to facilitate the processing of the Action Items that need solving.

1. **Scenario 1: Rapid-Fire Processing**

    a. Ask the owner of the Action Item the following questions:

        1. What have you done to date?

        2. What needs to be done?

        3. Where do you need help?

        4. From whom do you need help?

        5. What resources are needed to get the action item completed?

Quite often, you will be able to secure the necessary help and resources for the team member quickly and move on to the next item.

Example: Let's say a team member set the status of an Action Item to "H."

If the answers to questions 3 – 5 were: 3) I need a budget, 4) I need help from accounting to get it, and 5) I'll need to have these purchase orders executed in seven days to stay on track, then the issue could be resolved in minutes. The CFO could quickly assign the accounting resources, commit to determining the budget in two days, and commit to making sure the accounting team expedites the purchase orders.

2. **Scenario 2: Focused Processing**

Focused processing takes longer and requires more input from the group than an issue that qualifies for the Rapid Processing method. With focused processing, you will use a similar question set as those above to narrow the scope of the discussion. However, the discussion itself may be more complex.

Example: Let us say a team member set the status of an Action Item to "C." This means that something beyond their control impacted the Action Item, and it is not likely to be achieved without extra effort that was not planned. Ask these extra questions:

a. What changed?

b. What have you done to address the change?

c. What do you believe will be required to complete this Action Item on plan?

d. What help do you need from the group?

If the answers to these questions were: a) the warehouse burned down, b) not sure, c) a new warehouse, d) we need to determine if we are willing to build a new warehouse and also how to secure the necessary space now in order to hit our quarterly goal, assuming we can't build a warehouse in six weeks, then this would be a broader discussion for the group.

Let us go one step further: In answer "d," there were two questions. One question—whether building a new warehouse is possible, is strategic in nature. The second question regarding *getting space immediately* is tactical.

As the facilitator, you will want to assign the discussion about building a warehouse to the next strategic meeting while focusing the group on the tactical elements (budget, location, timeframe, etc.) of renting space as soon as possible.

6. Review the Decisions and Create New Projects (Action Items) – 5 minutes

After the discussions end, you will have new projects or action items listed on the whiteboard and, if using Catipult, you'll have a list in the notes section of the meeting in Catipult.

Quickly consolidate that work into Action Items and have each team member add their own action items with the due dates to their calendars or dashboards.

7. End and Score the Meeting

When the meeting is ready to end, use the same format for scoring your meeting as you would use to score a Weekly 80.

Leaving the Meeting

After scoring the meeting, give the team a reminder of what they just accomplished:

"Team, give yourself a round of applause. Seriously. Each of you came prepared for a four-hour meeting and crushed this meeting in just three hours. Meetings like this used to take all day. Great job!"

Optional Ending

Have the team read aloud, together, the company outcome statement. "The year is_____ and I am____"

"The year is ____ and we are _____"

Conclusion

Effective meetings take work and dedication. Follow this process. Trust it. It will deliver results.

The Catipult End-Of-Quarter Review Meeting
Rapid-Fire "Solve The Deltas"®

EOQ: The Strategic Workhorse

The End-of-Quarter (or simply, Quarterly) meeting is the strategic workhorse in the rhythm you're building. If you are coming from another system, you'll likely be surprised at how much you can get done using the format I'll illustrate here. Gone are the all-day sessions and prolonged discussions about random topics that frustrate everyone.

In the Quarterly, you're going to work on a logical construct that is better suited for the human brain's problem-solving abilities.

Other systems tend not to give people clear problems to solve in strategic meetings. With Catipult, the problems you need to solve are laid out in the system.

Solve The Deltas

Solving the deltas means that the executive team will be presented with KPIs deemed to be strategic in this meeting. The facilitator or coach will make sure to cover each one of those and solve the difference between the actual performance and the target goal for that KPI. You'll tackle this in a rapid-fire, 90-minute section of this meeting. Get ready to have fun.

Department Reporting

This meeting includes a fast-paced department-by-department reporting section on the agenda. You'll learn more about how to keep this part of the agenda item on pace below.

Facilitator Or Coach: Things To Consider

Most people enjoy the speed at which things get done using this format. However, there will be those on the executive team who like to talk... a lot. This format may run the risk of frustrating them. To that end, make sure you know your audience well. Identify those people and prepare them for a different style of meeting. Let them know that you, as the facilitator, will not be stopping the discussion, but rather focusing it like a magnifying glass focuses sunlight. You'll use the parking lot more than normal and possibly push some items into another meeting. Giving them advanced notice of the new meeting style will help them feel more prepared and less caught off guard.

One statement that's often fun to make at the introduction is: "This is going to be a fast-paced meeting. During this meeting, some of you will love me, then hate me. Others will first hate me, then love me. In the end, though, it will all be good."

Usually, this elicits a cautious laugh or two and breaks the ice.

In-Person Meeting Room Setting

The setting for the room is important. See the setting for Six-Week Tactical above.

Attire for an In-Person Meeting

The attire for the six-week tactical was comfortable. It is hard to require certain attire to be worn for any meetings, but if you have a team willing and able to play along, suggest that the team comes in business casual clothes. *This meeting needs to have a little more polish to it.*

Why? Psychologically, attire does set a mood. This is a strategic meeting, not a tactical meeting, and we want people's minds set up for planning before they even enter the room.

Meeting Virtually

If you are not able to get your team into one room for your Quarterly, one tool you may want to have available for a virtual meeting is a Miro board (www. miro.com). This is a great way to have the team collaboratively add sticky notes. They will be able to add to their own Catipult boards, spreadsheets, or calendars after the meeting and all notes will be in one accessible place.

Meeting Pre-Work

Like the Six-Week Tactical, there is no meeting pre-work beyond the normal updates the team is required to do before each of their weekly meetings.

- Have everyone update their KPI Actuals.

- Have your participants update their action items using the CHARP method.

- For all action items that are not checked in as on Plan, have them add notes directly to the action item.

- If they have issues to discuss that are not related to an action item in their plan, have them create a new issue and send it to this Quarterly

Meeting. (In Catipult this is easy: you can do it by choosing it from the drop-down menu in the Issues pop-up.)

Meeting Pre-Work for the Facilitator or Coach

To keep this meeting running at speed, review the plans and make sure only the KPIs that are considered strategic and important are in focus. Try limiting the KPIs to focus on for the quarterly to three. We'll discuss this number in more detail below.

If the facilitator or coach is not also the CEO, schedule a meeting with the CEO before this meeting to review the focus areas you have chosen. Make sure the CEO agrees. All other KPIs will be ignored.

Make sure the executive team is planning to attend this meeting and has updated their own KPIs and Action items.

You Driver Check-in – 10 minutes

Like the Tactical, start every meeting with a quick overview of how attendees are doing on at least one personal goal. Keep it quick—the maximum time allowed is only 10 minutes, regardless of the management team size.

Review the Mission, Vision, and Values – 5 minutes

Choose three volunteers for this exercise. Choose which one will read aloud the mission, vision, and value statements.

Report on Corporate (L1) KPIs not on Target – 15 minutes

First, make sure that you have those focus KPIs available. Doing this will display only the KPIs on which the company needs to focus in the next quarter. Follow these recommendations for the best results.

As I mentioned earlier, you should try to limit the focus KPIs discussed in this meeting ***to no more than three***. Why three? The process of selecting only three KPIs to cover is reflective and quite often will demand some sacrifice. The CEO and facilitator will have to discuss all the KPIs and choose three, which means they must justify at least to themselves why others should not be selected. Three helps define only the metrics most crucial to the company's success for the next quarter. With three, you will also get speed. Trying to

135

tackle more than three could become unwieldy. Think about it this way: would you rather solve the deltas for three KPIs, or solve nothing for all the KPIs?

As a bonus, the chance that you'll finish a meeting ahead of schedule is much more likely with three KPIs than five or six. If you finish ahead of schedule, then you can either give the team time back or choose to tackle another KPI. It doesn't hurt to have a fourth and fifth in your back pocket. Delivering strategic value on time is critical. If you are a third-party coach, you deliver value. If you're an internal facilitator, it won't take very many nonproductive Quarterlies for the CEO to say, "let's try to do this a different way," and you'll end up scrapping what others have used effectively. So be careful not to overload your agenda.

1. When picking your top three, pick a representative KPI from each of these three top business drivers:

   a. Employees

   b. Customers

   c. Cash or Growth

2. When choosing which KPI to select, place a priority on choosing from the core six KPIs. In some cases, other KPIs may be more important. For instance, a construction company may have a high rate of reported safety incidents, called TRIR. While TRIR is listed as a core world-class KPI for construction companies (that is, the Catipult system automatically recommends it for a construction company at the outset of setup), it is not one of the core six KPIs.

Departmental Reviews (L2) of KPIs Not on Target – 20 minutes

In this section, each department head reports their own KPIs and related action items. Department heads should also choose only three each to report to the team. *You will not solve the deltas for L2 KPIs in the strategic meeting.* Each department head should run this same agenda with their own team, they will have a team-only Quarterly where their three L2 KPIs will be the focus.

Report on Projects Completed Last Quarter – 10 minutes

During this time, you'll get to celebrate the "Done" box. Use this time as a positive moment for the team to review all the Action Items that they marked as "Done." Go around the room (or virtual room) and let people give each other high-fives, pats on the back, or other positive affirmations. The mood for this section should be very positive, even celebratory. You've been in the meeting for an hour. Take a five-minute break.

Discuss KPIs not on Target and Create Next Quarter's Projects – 90 minutes

We are now getting into the magic of running a world-class business. Your team members will experience something they've likely never experienced: speed and focus during a strategic meeting.

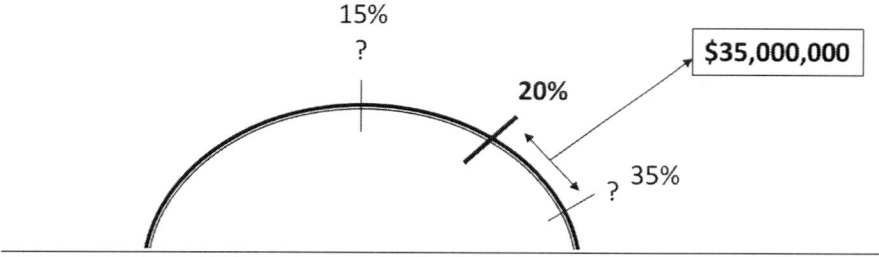

The next 90 minutes will be a rapid-fire discussion that will lead to "solving" the delta between the actual performance and the target metric. The graphic above (detailing the cost of having a concentration of revenue in one customer over 20 percent) reminds us of the vital importance just one KPI can have to the company.

Next, show them the seven business drivers. We call this the "Strategic Logic Tree." Make sure you show this at every meeting. Repetition creates expertise and will convert members of your team into world-class executives.

Go through the slide, explaining that you will review each of your three KPIs, and then, as a team, they will quickly identify, discuss, and choose action items/projects for the next quarter that will have an impact on the company's ability to achieve the target.

Because you are only working on corporate KPIs, multiple team members will be contributing solutions to each KPI. In the example above, you can see that sales, marketing, and engineering all created an action item to help drive the company toward Revenue Concentration KPI achievement.

Facilitating Per KPI – 30 minutes each

1. Pick the first KPI to tackle.

2. Highlight the delta: "We need to be at 20 and we are at 35." We are solving for 15. Write that down on the flip chart, tear that page off, and stick it to the wall.

Identify & Discuss – 15 minutes

3. Next, on one flip chart write: "worked," and on the other chart write, "didn't work."

4. Have each member of the team go to each board individually and write what worked about the action items that were associated with the KPI and what didn't work.

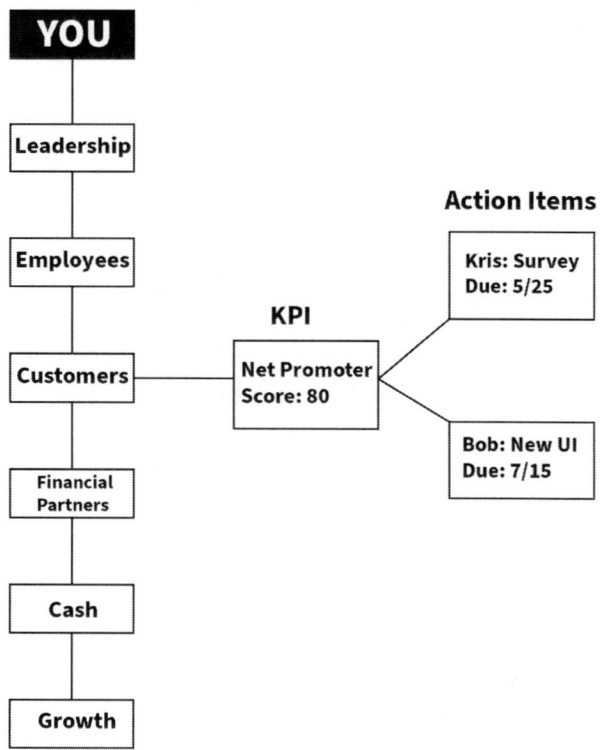

FOCUS ONLY ON THE ACTION ITEMS...This is not a session about what worked "in general."

Another way to phrase it is: "How did this / these action items help us toward our target and how did they not help us?"

5. Take a vote: Ask for a volunteer to read the "worked" and another to read the "didn't work." After each item has been read, ask for a show of hands of agreement and write the number of votes each one gets.

6. Circle the ones that had a plurality of team members agreeing. Example: *5/6 agreed Action Item A didn't work.*

7. Now, pick the two most important action items that the team agreed didn't work and ask them to name one reason each that they believe the project did not impact the KPI as expected. Write down those reasons as they are being mentioned.

Repeat Steps 1 – 7 three times, once for each KPI in rapid fire. If you have fewer than three focus KPIs, then you can extend the time for each one.

Solve – 10 minutes

8. Refer people to the worksheets. Instruct them to look at each and the reasons why the team believed a project didn't succeed as they move into this next step.

9. Have each member spend two minutes coming up with one or two major projects/action items that they and their department will own to help push the company along toward achieving the KPI target. Have them write down their dependencies – things that need to happen or help they need to get their action item done.

10. For the last five minutes, each team member tells the room the action items they created that they believe will help hit the company's targets.

General Issues Discussion – 20 minutes

By the time you have reached this agenda item, a lot of information has been flowing. You now have plans for each department that will hopefully contribute to the achievement of the corporate KPI or, at least, further progress toward it.

You can use this agenda space in four ways: 1) to discuss a pressing issue, 2) to extend the previous agenda item and have more time to review and discuss the next quarter's plans, 3) add a fourth KPI and run through it, 4) give everyone some time back.

End and Score the Meeting

Make sure that someone from the company has added the action items from the meeting into your system.

Score the meeting as discussed previously in the section on Weekly 80s.

Leaving the Meeting

You can use all the same techniques to wrap up a meeting as listed in previous sections on the Weekly 80 and the Six-Week Tactical.

Make sure you remind the team to have their own Quarterly with their reports.

Year End Review

The Year End Review is an all-day meeting, which you may want to do as an offsite.

Start up this meeting in the same way you begin some of the other meetings, with a 10-minute check in on the You Driver, and 5 minutes to review Mission, Vision and Values.

KPIs not on target – 35 minutes

Next, take 15 minutes to do a review of Corporate (L1) KPIs that are not on target yet, followed by 20 minutes to review L2 KPIs which are not on target.

State of the Market Review – 40 minutes

The end of the year is a great time to review things like market share, and market expansion or contraction, and to compare company market share to that growing or shrinking market at large. What else does your team need to know about the market in your particular industry? Include the most relevant questions and topics in your review; however, 40 minutes is plenty of time to give a thorough report. Like any good presentation, the presenter and facilitator may want to work together to think through how they can make this report both about the data and how it may impact the story the company wants to and needs to tell in the next year. Likely this "state of the market" review will be an Action Item for someone on the team to prepare for in the final quarter.

Adjusting KPIs

You don't want to change your KPIs every week! But once a year, take ten minutes to discuss whether or not the KPIs you set will actually help you hit your three-year outcome or not. If KPIs do need to be adjusted, now is the time to do it.

People Analyzer – 60 minutes

It's time to think through your key employees. The relationship between employee and employer changes over time, and sometimes people who were a fit a decade earlier are no longer a fit. On the other hand, people can grow into roles you'd never have imagined when they joined you at age twenty-three.

Here's a handy little tool called the People Guide. It is a nine-box exercise designed to help you determine where each person is in relationship to their ability to exercise the responsibilities that they currently have, and will have in the future, and should help you do it objectively. Oftentimes, we get in a room and one person might say, "Oh, I really love Charlotte, she needs to be promoted," but someone else will say, "I don't necessarily agree with that." If you're going to analyze people, do it while considering your three-year objectives and whether they're going to be able to help you get there. Do this together as an executive team. Put it up on a whiteboard and discuss each person based on the two major components of what's needed: adherence to values on the one hand, desire and ability to execute on the other. Get aligned as a team. You can also take that information and sit down with the employee to discuss where they stand. You don't need to show him or her where everybody else is on the map.

"We think you're amazing. And we think we can get you to this level, if you want it." And if they're open to that, a little bit more training, a little bit more leadership experience, whatever that is, then that employee may rise to the occasion. And you might have really done a great job for your culture. So the People Guide is not about firing. It's not about tearing people down. It's just the opposite. It's about seeing where people are, and making sure that you as a leadership team, and as an owner or CEO, know where they're at. You can build them up if they need to be built up and reward them if they're already there. But you do have to make sure that you've got the right team to get where you want to go.

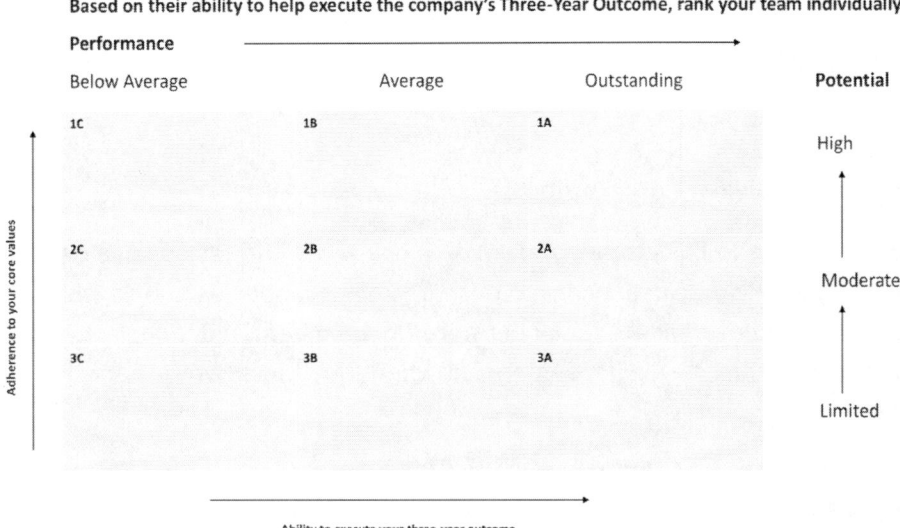

Based on their ability to help execute the company's Three-Year Outcome, rank your team individually.

There are two major considerations for whether people continue to be a good fit on your team. I like to use a chart with nine segments. On one axis, we rank people according to how well they fit the mission, vision and values of the company. Do they embody the values in a way that's subpar, average, or excellent? On the other axis is the combination of the desire and ability to perform. Do they have both huge desire and the ability to excel, are they average, or below average in desire and ability?

The person who has both a high adherence to values, high desire and ability to perform, ranks in the upper right quadrant, while the person who is low on both axes goes in the lower left.

Thought Provokers:

1. Explain your ranking criteria. How did you arrive at your conclusions?

2. If any of your rankings are different than the most recent employee reviews, what has changed?

3. In what ways could keeping low performers (Rows 2 & 3) in their current positions impact the ability to achieve the outcome?

4. How can you be sure your high performers are going to stay?

5. What is the plan to "deepen" the bench to de-risk the event that high performers leave?

6. What training programs are in place and not working as planned to bring low performers to a higher level?

7. Which, if any, employees on your team are impacting (positively or negatively) other departments and projects?

8. What are action items that you're now considering after this exercise?

Running the People Guide on Your Executive Team

Nobody cares about your business as much as you do. You may want to use this tool to analyze your executive team, who will be helping you to analyze all your L3, 4 and 5 employees. If you need to run this exercise on the leadership team, this is a great time to have a conversation with a third-party coach, someone who can help you remain objective as you discuss your challenges with your L2 group. This way, you can also have kind, considerate conversations with them about places where you feel there's a lack of pizzazz in their connection to your values or drive and ability to perform.

Process Analyzer – 60 minutes

Processes are the things that move business forward. Without a process, you might be operating an organization that stalls out or lacks any rhythm, it is helter skelter. But when we're looking at our three-year outcome and the vision that we have for our company, we really have to take a deep dive routinely on the processes that we have in place, especially at the beginning of your three-year journey, because the process that you have now may not be the ones that can scale you to where you want to be. Processes you have now may not actually be working, you might not have some processes in place at all for certain things. It's easy to say, "These things we're doing don't make any sense, but we've been doing it that way for 20 years. So why change?" Well, here's the reason you want to change: the past doesn't exist; instead, you are beginning a journey for the next three years. The worksheet is pretty simple.

List all the processes for each one of the seven business drivers. Now, why did we do it in terms of business drivers, and not in terms of functions like marketing, operations, finance? Well, here's the reason: many departments contribute to each of the business drivers. You want to see where that contribution is and how things overlap. If we just look at marketing and check out the marketing functions or sales and check out the sales functions, we might miss some overlaps, we might miss some very important handoffs, we might not even recognize the fact that maybe there should be some handoffs that don't exist, that can make things more efficient.

So go through this exercise:

List all your processes with everything that contributes to generating cash. List every process that contributes to growth. List every process that contributes to employee engagement, including training, continuing education, hiring and retention. List every process in your organization that contributes to customer satisfaction, and healthy and excited financial partners.

Once you list all of those things, you'll see how each of the departments has roles and functions that contribute to each of those drivers.

It will be eye-opening. Next, you'll see which processes are the ones you need to tackle first. I don't recommend you tackle more than one per quarter. Tackling a process can be a big ordeal for an organization. So don't over commit and stress yourself out. Pick the most important process that feels broken or that needs to be created. Work on that for the first quarter and then pick another one and then another one. Continue to iterate and look at these processes.

I recommend the book, *The E-Myth.* It talks about creating the processes that will run your organization, and how to do so as well as many franchises are run. Franchises are among the most successful and longest running businesses that we have. Why is that? Processes. If they can do it, you can do it.

Brainstorm on what needs to be done in the next year – 60 minutes

Get into a creative mindset here and allow your three-year outcome to spark your imagination. What else could you do to make things happen that you aren't already doing? Do you need to explore and completely reinvent something? Or do you just need to tweak and iterate a process? The facilitator should invite any and all suggestions and make sure to cut people off when they say "but we can't do that because..." Stay in that brainstorming mode.

You may want to start with a creative exercise, like an improv challenge or drawing with crayons. Some other great tools include a Miro Board or a Futures Wheel exercise.

Narrow down the projects for the first quarter – 60 minutes

Once you have lots of ideas, you can put your analytical brain back to work. Get the team to figure out which of your various projects ought to take precedence and prioritize your top five.

It's important to remember that your three-year plan is just that: a three-year plan, not a one-quarter plan, so be sure not to overload your team with special projects on top of their regular work. Rome was not built in a day, and neither was your company. Yes, we're all about World-Class Speed, and we were able to do that using a Three-Year Outcome and the six most important KPIs to change the direction your business was heading in the first week, but there are other things that will take time.

A coach or facilitator should recognize which things require action immediately when implementing the process I've outlined in this book, and which things will take at least half of the 36-month period you're working on. Working at World-Class Speed doesn't mean you don't need to exercise patience as well, so find that balance in this 60-minute segment of your annual meeting.

Score your meeting and conclude – 5 minutes

Discussions

By now you have probably noticed that while running your meetings, you have had little time for sidebar discussions. You've kept your team on task in each meeting, and no doubt after thirteen Weekly 80s, one Six-Week Tactical, and one Quarterly, there were plenty of things that your team didn't have time to tackle. These things needed more discussion, but you were disciplined and put them off to the side.

We used to call Discussions "Issues," but many CEOs gave me feedback indicating that "issues" had a negative connotation for themselves and their team.

Has someone ever said to you something like, "Hey, Janet, I have an issue on the Barnes Project we need to talk about," and you thought, *"Oh, no, what did I do wrong?"* Consider these more positive comments instead:

"Hey Janet, could we have a discussion about a possible **redirect** on the Barnes Project next Monday?"

"Hey Janet, could we have a discussion next week about ways that we could **help** each other on the Barnes Project?"

"Hey Janet, could we have a discussion when you get back about a **change** that Gary over at Barnes Inc. wants to make on their project?"

"Hey Janet, I want to make sure you're **aware** of our team's progress on the Barnes Project, could we do a five-minute discussion next week?"

None of these leaves you worrying about or losing sleep all weekend over the Barnes Project, does it?

Since language matters, we've readjusted from "Issues" and began to call these items "Discussions."

What is a Discussion? Typically, when something is marked "Aware" it's possible that a discussion is warranted; and some discussions are not about solving problems, but have more to do with strong communication, letting people know what's going on, or perhaps, in some cases, letting people know what you're thinking about.

When beginning a "Discussion", participants should always clarify the hoped-for outcome of the discussion first. Does something need to be fixed? Is a solution required? If so, perhaps the item ought to be marked "Help". If the discussion is to raise awareness, that's all it is. Stick to the point: "I'm aware that Janice is going on maternity leave next month and that means our department will need to pick up some slack."

"I'm concerned about the trend in our market; we're gaining market share, but overall volume of linoleum is down, while bamboo flooring is on the upswing. We don't need to solve anything today, but I'd like to discuss possible options for how we might address this trend in the next quarter."

Making people aware of your thoughts is good communication, inviting them into your panic, not so much. Your panic does not need to become the company picnic.

The great thing about the CHARP system within a solid meeting structure is that you can stay on task. If someone needs to have a discussion but it would be a sidebar for most of the people in the meeting, create a "Discussion" and *invite only those to whom it is relevant.*

Don't waste time in meetings discussing items that don't yet need to be solved with people who don't need to be there. Meetings are the biggest drain on productivity in all corporate settings, no matter whether they are small businesses, medium, large, or enterprise level.

Once your team gets the hang of running meetings like the Weekly 80, the Six-Week Tactical, and the Quarterly, the next challenge to conquer is for them to also have Discussions that stick to the point.

Industry Expert Interviews And Case Studies:

Jen Hamilton

Masterful Meetings

I've been running meetings for over 25 years. So, I can speak to what has happened with different companies by just having productive, focused meetings. It's only been the last two years or so that I've been leading meetings in a productive, focused fashion, as a fractional COO and it makes a world of difference.

When I'm selling coaching, I've noticed that even in the sales process, my prospect is already thinking, "Oh my gosh, we're going to have more meetings? The last thing we need is more meetings!" But the way they think about meetings, they're not productive, effective, or focused. And that's often true. Most meetings are unproductive unless they have a formal structure like we have with Catipult.

What I often saw was what I'd call an "update" meeting. It included people who don't need to be there. It's just a waste of time. You can do the math: If you take all their hourly rates and you multiply by the number of hours, the number of weeks and so on, are you getting a return on your investment? Most people would say "no."

The idea of having weekly meetings and one-on-one meetings at first often turns clients off, because they usually did it wrong. They still left a lot of time for updates.

They'd ask, "What's going on with that project?" when it didn't need to be discussed. In a lot of unproductive meetings, people spend a lot of time on things that are on track because there hasn't been a communication system for the leadership to know what's happening with their team.

Having meetings via Catipult has been very helpful, but better yet, with Catipult, at any point in the week you don't have to have a meeting to know what's going on. A leader can go in and see what the status of their KPIs is, the status of their action plans, what is it that they're working on… without having to have a meeting just to find out what's on plan. That's the biggest shift I would say from other systems is that you don't have to have a meeting *at all* to get updates. With my clients, instead of having more meetings, we're doing fewer of them.

The shift required to make meetings productive includes two main points. One, it's time to focus on what you need to focus on (the KPIs). Two, clarity and transparency of the status of different things. If it's on plan, then you don't need to dive in. But what do you do if it's not on plan? For example, if you need feedback from the team so you can move forward, or if you need a new decision, or if you need best practice or some research, or there's an obstacle in the way, keeping the team from moving forward, whether it's the leaders or the folks on their team, then yes, you need to have that meeting.

Setting aside time in the Weekly 80 and even doing the same format in a one-on-one gives you most of the time to solve, discuss, and move things forward. And to me, that's where I think the combination of focusing truly on just what you need to know and what you need to fix has allowed for my clients to… catapult … their results and get things done much quicker than they thought.

Law Firm On Exponential (But Messy) Growth Track

I recently worked with a large and growing law firm. They went from three people to 30 people within two years. One of the things they chose to do was put in another operating system, but they didn't fully implement it. When I came in and observed a leadership team meeting for the first time, while I was assisting them in a transition from one COO to the next, I was able to see where they invested most of their time as a leadership team. They were getting into the weeds and trying to get all the details covered, and not everyone needed to be a part of that conversation. Some of the feedback that I received after that first meeting from the leaders included the fact that they didn't really feel like EOS was useful and weren't excited about me coming in and leading more of these meetings.

The next week I started running these meetings in a more focused way. I'd say, "Okay, that sounds like that's a departmental decision. Let's make that a task for them to work on, and can you schedule something for you guys to work on offline as a team and then bring back your decision to the next meeting?" Instantly they realized, "Oooh, we don't have to discuss everything here! Let's just move forward. It doesn't have to be fully figured out with this whole team sitting here, wasting time."

After a few months of this, the most resistant person said to me, "Jen, I have to give you credit, because I hated our leadership meetings. They were a huge waste of time. And since you came in, I have looked forward to them. I feel like we're moving the company forward. We're not just spinning our wheels."

So, we actually got quite a few projects done and were able to make some significant changes in their culture, getting the wrong people out of the wrong seats, and dealing with a load of client complaints until the complaints decreased significantly. We were able to focus on marketing strategy and overarching planning. Instead of working in their own little silos, they started to work together. So, all these things were able to lead to a stronger, better team and culture.

And then they were able to have a clear pathway for appropriate growth. So while they were shrinking at first, now they are able to grow smarter. Instead of just throwing bodies at problems (which is what they were doing when they grew from three to 30) now they were growing with the right people and were able to sustain that growth, as well as reduced complaints and increased client loyalty and referrals. It all started with better meetings.

Dental Practice Consultants

A less dramatic example comes from an organization providing consulting and coaching services in the dental industry. They didn't want to grow fast but went from three on the team up to five. They had been doing the typical update meetings. I met with them recently and I was really pleased. They used to have a terrible habit of spending half of the meeting doing updates. Over time, we've been able to help them focus. We've added data: they never looked at data before. And now we're starting to see consistent growth in areas where they never had it before. They're getting referrals, that's where most of their growth comes from. They have consistently been adding upsells to their current clients, which they never did before, by having that as a focus.

All of our action steps are now tied into KPIs. I started with them in February 2022, and by the end of December, it was the best revenue year they had ever had. And then this year, it's on the same path, and they now have more clients at a higher revenue level than they've ever had before. They're growing slow and smart, by design. The founder doesn't want to grow a huge firm. But in the last two months, they added two full-time service providers, because they've added so many new clients and new service offerings too.

What's fun is seeing these clients help their dental office clients run their meetings better, and bringing these practices to their clients, and getting a ripple effect of referrals.

It has been exciting to see a little tortoise running the race and then also compare it to the hare running the race, and both of these clients are doing great just by having better meetings.

CHAPTER 9: PEOPLE

"The system runs the business. The people run the system."

— Michael E. Gerber, *The E-Myth Revisited*: Why Most Small Businesses Don't Work and What to Do About It

In this chapter, we're going to discuss people. We added them last because leading people and managing processes should only happen after the plan is built and objectives clearly stated.

Before we dive too deeply into this topic, let's address you and your role as an owner in the company. In his book *E-Myth*, Micheal Gerber identifies three primary personalities in a company: the entrepreneur, manager, and technician. While it is tempting to develop my own system, since Gerber nailed it; it's not necessary.

According to Gerber, an entrepreneur is also a dreamer, a thinker, a storyteller, and a leader who can inspire others to join their vision.[9]

Gerber contrasts the entrepreneur with two other types of business personalities: the technician and the manager. The technician is focused on doing the technical work of the business, such as making, selling, or delivering the product or service. The technician is often skilled and passionate about their craft but may not have the strategic or managerial skills to grow the business beyond their own capacity. The manager is responsible for organizing and controlling the business operations, such as planning, budgeting, hiring, and supervising. The manager is often pragmatic and efficient but may not have the creative or visionary skills to innovate or differentiate the business from the competition.

Gerber argues that most small businesses are started by technicians who suffer from an entrepreneurial seizure, meaning that they decide to create their own job without understanding what it takes to build a successful business. He claims that this is the main reason why many small businesses fail or struggle to survive. He suggests that to create a business that works, the owner needs to shift their perspective from working **in** the business to working **on** the business. This means that they need to transcend their own personality and role and develop the skills and mindset of all three personalities: the entrepreneur, the manager, and the technician.

What I've seen with the other models that use concepts like "visionary" and "integrator" is that owners grab hold of the nice title of "visionary" and the idea of getting an "integrator" without fully embracing the mindset of all three roles that Gerber highlights. Furthermore, just because someone is at the top or started a company, does not mean that they are visionary. In some cases, the results of this mentality can be disastrous. Owners embraced the title with too much gusto and believed they were the only ones with a vision and treated their integrators as if they could only manage operations and not really handle strategy.

Granted, the human ego has strange triggers. This highlights another example of the principle that words matter.

The Challenge With Both Concepts

What Gerber doesn't say is described in his graphic, which has the entrepreneur on top. In similar fashion, the concept of visionary also rests at the top of the food chain. But, what if they don't?

What happens when a company is run by a perfectionist with little penchant for vision and the true visionary works for the CEO? Or the technician can't adapt, but managed to hire an entrepreneur? Should they switch titles?

I've spent a few decades in technology, which is long enough to know that engineers, who are founders and CEOs, find it difficult to make the leap to entrepreneur. While they do have a vision for the future, they are not often the ones who can develop it beyond the initial product or have a vision for the company. There's nothing wrong with this, it just is.

Keeping It Simple

Let's not complicate business by creating new titles and ideas that can't possibly span the breathtaking depth of human personality and the traits that ebb and flow as various situations and stimuli are presented.

As an owner, that's your title. Your objective is eventually to own the business and not to run it. To meet that objective, you may hire an executive team. You may choose to hire a fractional COO or full-time COO. You may choose to hire a president. At any given time, you may choose to hand the entire company over to someone to run. Or you may choose not to do so.

There's no one right way to do you. So, let's not pretend there is.

Your Goal: Own The Business, Don't Be An Employee Of It

As Socrates famously said, "know thyself." When you know yourself, you can hire for your weaknesses. With the stated goal above, we can start to develop an organization structure and hiring strategy or evaluate the one you already have. Here are a few steps to get you started.

1. As an owner, envision yourself spending five hours per week with "this" business (your current one). Use that term to create a degree of separation from where you may mentally be now. "I'm spending five hours a week on this business," not "My business." What does that look like?

2. Create a list of your weaknesses. Yes, you have them. Did you hire a team that's stronger than you in your weakest areas or did you hire clones of yourself? The latter won't get you to the five-hour work week. That list of weaknesses becomes the initial list of job requirements and functions. Even if you have a great team in place, this exercise is still very helpful. It often exposes an area where you could hire for a delta.

3. Evaluate that list and see if anything on it represents a functional area or simply a skill set. For example, "I'm weak at lead generation" may be an opportunity to hire a marketing head. You may also find that the person you hired was chosen because you liked the conversations you had with them, and they also can't run lead generation. If you like marketing strategy, hiring someone like you will only create the need to hire a third person—the one that will execute the strategy. I've seen this many times. Ultimately, the owner usually won't let go of strategy because that's their talent but does fire the clone to make room for someone who will simply do it.

4. Create a list of everything you do. Once that list is created, assign everything to the team you have in place—on paper. Don't start assigning it to them right away. If you can't assign it all, then look at the remaining items on the list and begin to think of the positions that need to be hired to do all that was left.

5. Run the same play with the team you have in place. Have them create a list of everything they do and what they would need to get off their plate to take over everything you do.

6. Start parsing this list into functions and roles/titles in an org-chart format. You may have areas with no description or title. That's okay... at least create catch-all boxes that you can review later.

7. Check your outcome statement. What do you think will be needed to hit the objectives there? Don't be surprised if the answer is "not much." Once you get through the first six steps, you're left with a list of all the functions a company likely has and you'll only need to add scalability to hit your outcome.

I'm a seven on the Enneagram personality scale. That's affectionately called the "shiny object" personality. We're creative, fun, spontaneous and have a lot of ideas. I also have ADHD, which allows me to do many things at once and build companies quickly. It also means my brain collapses when it gets into a structure, routine, or God-forbid, something I must interact with—*details* (I could barely type that word). You're probably sensing some irony right now. How did my personality type ever produce a system and structure that others are using? Good question.

When building and scaling my companies, I had to be honest with myself and realize that my long-term success ultimately depends on my ability to hire someone who is the exact opposite of me. With Catipult, I hired a hard-charging Enneagram eight with a love for process and details and a passion for building both fast. She, not I, runs the Catipult process in my company, Catipult.ai. Her title is President and Chief Operating Officer. Her functional role is running all aspects of the company where routine and attention to detail are paramount. She's both a manager, tactician, and entrepreneur as she brings creativity and vision to our operations. I would never call myself the visionary or her just an integrator of my vision.

My role will evolve as the company does and one day soon, I'll be acting as the owner, spending five hours per week working on the company and less than that working in it.

People

When discussing the Employee Driver, I touched on Richard Branson's key to success: employees first, and promised that we'd come back around for a deeper look into the question "What does it look like to focus on employees?" Here's a checklist of items that, if in place, will help transform your culture and increase productivity, accountability, and retention.

- Communicate your vision and goals to everyone in the company clearly. Over-communicate them. Hang signs around your office, mention them in every all-hands meeting, town hall, Weekly 80, Six-Week Tactical, Quarterly and even in Discussions.

- Benchmark your company performance against your goals on a regular basis. Tell employees where you are, relative to sales, product development, hiring, etc. Make them part of the solution.

- Hold yourself and your management team accountable for not canceling meetings with their teams. Frequent cancellations and rescheduled meetings are disrespectful to the human beings who are on the other end, and create a culture where people cancel on each other as a matter of routine. Canceling meetings, especially at the last minute, is a productivity killer! Like a race car on the track at the Indianapolis 500®, skipping pit stops means losing traction.

- Allow employees to create measurable goals for themselves and tie them into their own personal and professional objectives. (If it stands to reason that your life starts with you, then so do the lives of your employees.) Then, hold them accountable for achieving their business goals. Build incentive programs around accountability—and stick to them.

- Quickly fire the bottom ten percent of employees who don't "get with the program." This is a strategy from Jack Welch, the former CEO of General Electric. Firing the bottom feeders respects those employees who are putting in the time for your company and increases morale. Keeping underperformers on the payroll only brings everyone else down. As a result, your top performers leave. Once that begins, it won't be long before you see an avalanche of talent headed toward the door, while those who are not getting with the program will stick around and draw a paycheck for as long as you'll allow them to do so.

- Hold regular team-building events and build your own traditions. Don't schedule them if you're not serious about rhythms. Don't cancel these events, either! This could be a Thursday free lunch day or something else. Having your own traditions will help people bond around your company. But traditions are for more than just bonding. Traditions are for celebrating progress. At the Indianapolis 500, the winner gets showered with milk. At the Master's golf tournament in Augusta, the winner gets a green jacket. Why? Well, it hardly matters anymore, does it? If you won one of those events and walked away with the paycheck but didn't get bathed in milk or didn't get to don the green jacket, it would feel like you got cheated somehow. We are social animals, and our traditions matter just as much, or more, than money.

Your employees are more important than your customers. In fact, you are your employees' customer. They sell you the better part of their time and energy every day. Don't take them for granted! Make sure you're paying them better than the industry average or at least on par with the average. If you're below average, you'd better have one heck of a fantastic work environment or a great purpose statement that makes people want to stay! This is how non-profits keep their executives, but even so, they must be somewhat comparable to for-profit executive pay. (According to one report, at least nine CEOs at nonprofits in the USA were paid a salary of over $10 million in 2022.[10])

Resignations are important to monitor. There's obviously something going on if the resignations begin to skyrocket. In today's environment, people can be highly engaged one day... and then they're out the door the next day because they just got a call from a headhunter or an old friend or former colleague, offering 20 percent to 30 percent more income. So, you're going to want to monitor your salaries and make sure that your key players are always being paid either higher than everybody else is paying or at least on par to make sure you keep them.

But pay isn't the only factor in employee engagement, it's just scratching the surface. Smart people know when the grass isn't greener on the other side, and they'll stay with you even when offered higher pay, if they're engaged in a variety of ways. On the other hand, if your employees are well compensated but aren't engaged in other ways, it is only a matter of time before you could have a turnover problem– with people leaving for equal or even lower pay! Once that happens, it may be too late! You don't want to end up in a vicious cycle of paying too much overtime or spending crazy amounts of cash constantly trying to hire and train, (both of which are terrible for your EBITDA or Burn KPI) while people leave as fast as you can burn them out.

Stay ahead of the quitting or "quiet quitting" curve by tracking engagement. Depending on your industry there could be a variety of factors. The Owner or CEO doesn't need to drill down into the details every week, but they should be given one simple overall score on a regular basis that gives them a bigger picture view; if the score indicates a problem they can drill down if necessary.

While developing an overall Employee Engagement score, you may want to track things like:

- Resignations: Is your pay competitive against the industry standards?

- Rewards and recognition. Don't hinge your entire engagement strategy on handing out trophies when people complete their 25th year at your company! While it is true that awards and appreciation, bonuses and raises, are important, according to Dan Pink in his seminal work *Drive*, the three keys to motivation (assuming an employee is compensated a livable wage) are mastery, autonomy, and purpose.

- How much do people feel appreciated? (If the answer indicates that your company culture is not strong in this area, *The 5 Languages of Appreciation in the Workplace* by Gary Chapman & Paul White could be a great resource.) Are they getting affirmed verbally in an authentic way?

- What percentage of your workforce is getting additional training which could lead toward promotions? (Mastery)

- How much do people feel they're given opportunities to take ownership and work without micromanagement? (Autonomy)

- Sense of Purpose – on a scale of 1-10, how much do they think what they do every day makes a difference in the world?

- Productivity and workload balance.

- Employee health (physical and mental: fatigue, burnout).

- Are people using their paid time off and vacation, or do they feel pressure not to use them? (Easily tracked by percentage of vacation days used.) If you're in the USA, take a hint and compare the satisfaction of the workforces in Europe, where taking your vacation time is much more culturally acceptable.

- Net Promoter Score - One question survey: on a scale of 1-10, how likely would your employee be to recommend your business as a place to work for a friend?

- A survey with the focus on key employees, your executive team, of course, but this also might include critical positions within your organization that have zero redundancy, for example: the only employee who knows how to operate or repair a particular, complicated machine or process. Don't overlook the people who could bring your entire workflow to a halt if they decided not to show up for a week (and if you have anyone like that, it's probably time to start training someone else to create the redundancy you're missing).

Ask your human resources leadership to develop their own set of more precise KPIs to drill down on the most relevant aspects of your employee engagement. They can use any of the bullet points listed above and add in things that are unique to your business, to create a customized Employee Engagement score for the CEO.

Every group of friends has that person who loves to grill meat. Perhaps that's you – imagine it with me even if you're a vegetarian: You've experienced hamburgers since you got your first grill when you were twenty-three. Twenty times every summer (and even a few times in winter) you start up with a variety of rubs, spices, sauces, and seasonings and you slather and slop, you flip and flop, until aaaaah, just right, it's medium, just the way you like it, and hmm, a different flavor than ever before. Most of the time you surprise yourself– in a good way– with what you've done. You don't write down recipes, you go by the feel of it, and everyone who comes to the barbecue says it's the best burger they've ever had.

Now consider McDonalds. As we've discussed previously, they don't hire chefs, innovators, or experimental foodie philosophers... visionaries. They hire kids who have never cooked a burger before, in fact, it doesn't even matter if they can read the words "microwave popcorn". McDonalds has a system– and it is not designed to turn kids into chefs or foodies. It's a system that runs the business, and then they hire sixteen and seventeen-year-old kids to run the system.

"But we want to be World-Class," you say, "So we do custom work."

Even within the world of custom work, such as an Amish custom kitchen cabinet woodworking shop, there are people who run their business based on systems and there are people who fly by the seat of their pants. If nothing else, a custom shop needs a system to tell them whether a project they are bidding on will be profitable, and a system to streamline even the cutting of custom-sized parts. How you stack parts, and where you stack them, matters on project number one, and matters even more as you scale. There are several reasons why people might balk at the implementation of new systems. But "We've always done it this way!" is not an excuse, especially when 'always done it this way' means 'we've never been consistent before, why should we do that now?'

But while people love to judge systems, the truth is that numerical systems can also make it much easier to evaluate human performance. Think about this: why do people spend hours of their lives on the Internet arguing whether Dale Murphy or Tommy John ought to be in the baseball Hall of Fame? Because they have statistics! In every argument, multiple metrics are listed! If you've been evaluating performance subjectively, all sorts of problems can come into play. The worst-case scenario is a wrongful termination or discrimination lawsuit, nightmares for any business no matter how frivolous the suit is. At best, subjectivity is a subtle way to install nepotism or cronyism.

"Because I like you..." is not the best way to select someone for a promotion, in fact, it may be the worst. If it's true that people rise to the level of their own incompetence, this may be due in some cases to "because I like you," but what is the reason they stay in a position where they lack competence? The answer is that the lack of metrics makes it very difficult to remove someone from their position.

Baseball is easy. Pitchers come and pitchers go. It's nothing personal, but if they give up more runs than someone who can replace them, it's over. If you're going to pay an executive the same wage as a Major League Baseball player at minimum salary ($720,000) or even half or a quarter of that amount, why wouldn't you evaluate their performance statistically, the same way a major league ball club's general manager does?

Get rid of bias and noise, take the friendly relationship out of the equation, and focus on attaining KPIs. Why? Because these factors can and will undermine employee morale, hinder equitable recognition, and create dissonance within teams over the long term. The introduction of KPIs addresses these concerns by introducing an objective and data-driven approach to employee assessment.

Making the Shift to KPI-based Evaluation

There's going to be pushback. It's human nature to resist change.

You have a few options immediately. One option is to check in on adaptability. Someone resisting KPIs may be telling you they aren't very adaptable; if this is the case, you may be able to help them.

Ross Thornley, CEO of AQai, says, "Adaptability has two parts. The National Institute for Health issued a paper in 2015 describing it 'as a disposition and skill – adaptability is essential to an individual's psychological health, social success and academic or workplace achievement.' So in that context, adaptability is super important. A couple of years earlier, there was a quote saying, 'adaptability is the capacity to adjust one's thoughts and behaviors in order to effectively respond to uncertainty, new information and changed circumstances.' Now, that has become part of the lexicon because of the pandemic. Whilst it's always been there and it's part of our evolution, now it's critical. The other factor of what AQ is, and this is a term that in the last ten years has just started to become something, is the *metric of adaptability.*"[11]

Yes, even adaptability has metrics!

So, while someone who is resistant to metrics may be telling you they aren't very adaptable, (which can be improved), they may also be telling you that they're flat-out lazy: they don't know how to do the work, don't want to learn, and most of all, don't want their incompetence to be exposed. Therefore, sometimes the best thing you can do is recognize that someone is sitting in the wrong seat.

It may not be very common, but is it so terrible to offer someone their old job back? A demotion, a pay cut, sure, but think about it: if your star saleswoman got promoted to sales manager and started messing everything up, and a year later your sales are down, firing her might not be the best option – the best option may be to re-position her where she used to shine. In fact, you might offer some new KPIs to give her a chance to earn more than she was previously when she was crushing it in outbound sales. If that's a possibility, why fire her? Unfortunately, due to the current impact of the broader business culture, employees may be socially embarrassed to take on a role which their friends and family might see as a demotion, and they may decide to leave anyway.

So, when you begin to use KPIs and people struggle, some of the options (perhaps not a complete list) are to:

1. Help them adapt to the new systems (and use metrics to prove their adaptability is increasing).

2. Reposition them where they have proven to be competent.

3. Gently terminate their employment (or graciously accept their resignation).

No matter how you decide to deal with the transition, it's a proven fact: KPIs provide a standardized framework that ensures fairness and consistency across evaluations. This transparency enhances trust between employees and management.

Not only are KPIs valuable in determining whether the right butts are in the right seats, they can also be used for compensation and bonuses.

Because there's nothing people love more than to know exactly what is

164

expected and required of them (giving them a very real sense of security), the direct link between KPIs and compensation and bonuses serves as a powerful incentive for outstanding performance.

By aligning financial rewards with quantifiable KPIs, you can create a results-driven culture that nurtures employee motivation, productivity, and commitment. Be aware, however, that motivation is tied to far more than money.

Establishing a symbiotic relationship between KPIs and compensation strategies has some obvious benefits:

Merit-Based Compensation: Linking compensation and bonuses to KPIs ensures that rewards are commensurate with an employee's actual contributions. This approach mitigates disparities arising from tenure-based compensation systems by implementing clear performance expectations.

Continuous improvement mindset: KPIs that influence compensation encourage employees to strive for excellence, embrace creativity, innovation, and adaptability, and continually seek ways to enhance their performance. Designing a KPI to empower employees toward autonomy in decision making is one of the most important things a CEO can do to begin to break away from the CEO-centric pattern that keeps you constantly on call, unable to spend a month at the cabin or a week on a cruise. Make sure to develop KPIs that reward innovative thinking.

Don't forget that after you "Start with YOU," the employees are your next most important group to consider– not your customers! Therefore, your KPIs should be designed with Employee Engagement and Retention in mind. This will make a difference for those working for you today and will attract other high performers to your system. As the employees go, so goes the organization: As individual employees align their efforts with KPIs, overall organizational performance will improve. When every employee's work contributes to measurable results, collective success is virtually guaranteed.

Defining Appropriate KPIs

KPIs should align with the organization's goals. They should be specific, measurable, achievable, relevant to your core values, and time-bound (SMART), providing a robust framework for evaluation. Strike a balance between multiple KPIs. Avoid overemphasizing one aspect over others. At the same time, too many KPIs are overwhelming.

Rhythm, in terms of KPIs, means regular evaluation and feedback: Constant communication is key to a successful KPI-driven compensation system. Regular performance evaluations (certainly more often than the typical "Six Month Review") and feedback sessions ensure employees remain aligned with their goals and understand the impact of their contributions.

Flexibility: Humans need to be adaptable, but so do KPIs. Organizations must be flexible in adjusting KPIs as priorities shift or new challenges emerge.

Fairness and Transparency: The compensation structure must be fair and transparent, ensuring employees understand how their performance influences their rewards. Clear communication builds trust and minimizes confusion.

Chapter 10: Catipult Coaching - the Glue Between Immutable KPIs and Meeting Excellence

In this chapter, you'll find:

- For business owners: Why you need an external coach

- How to select the coach who is right for you

- Where to find a coach

- For coaches: How to become a Catipult coach

Why Hire An External Coach?

"Why should I get a coach? Coaching takes time, and I don't have any." You wouldn't be the first business owner to say this, nor will you be the last. What if I told you that a good coach will *save you eight hours a week?!* Yes, of course there's time invested up front, but isn't that the case with any system you've ever implemented to save time and money later on down the road? The first reason to hire a coach is to save time. Will it save you money? Think of the costly mistake that one client made which he didn't realize until he went to the bank to evaluate his business and found that his business was worth $35 million less than he thought, because of his customer concentration being over 20 percent. Now, if a coach is charging you $35 million you might be overpaying... but yes, somewhere along the line, a good coach is going to save you money. Possibly millions. Coaching isn't a luxury item for people who have too much time on their hands and a head full of existential crisis. It's an investment. Get your time back, avoid costly mistakes. Those are the top two reasons to hire a coach.

What about accountability? A business owner recently mentioned that he wasn't going to pay $XXX per hour for accountability. We agree. Healthy accountability is voluntary, and in the ideal setting, you can be accountable to the people you lead. I'm accountable to my children (not my parents) to take care of my finances so I can pass on generational wealth. I'm accountable for my pipeline, to my workforce to make sure we have enough work for the assembly line, because they're depending on a paycheck to feed their families. Accountability is to those you serve by leading, not to your coach. That said, there may be some ways a good coach can help you be accountable. For example, everybody wants something from you. Your coach may be the only person who will advocate for you and remind you that you must "Start with You."

Everyone else has an agenda for you: your spouse wants more of your time, more money, or both. Your executive team wants your input, expects your leadership. Your vendors and customers have an agenda; they want to get more for less... and even your best networking partners, people who send you referrals, well, they do want you to send them referrals in return.

It would not quite be accurate to say that an external coach has no agenda, or wants nothing: they need to be paid, yes, and they'd love to have referrals, too. But a good coach has both the training and the discipline to make your agenda their agenda. They will offer principles, sure, just as I am offering principles throughout this book, but how to apply them in your business– that's your department.

One of the first things you may want to do with a coach is to review your three-year outcomes, your driver and KPIs, your business's core values, vision and mission statements. In fact, you may want to do this in tandem with a coach even before you start tinkering around in Catipult. Your coach should have the skills to ask probing questions to help you sharpen, hone and simplify your statements. If you already have these things dialed in pretty well, it will still be good for your coach to know them and be able to point you back to them if you start heading off on a tangent.

You'll notice that throughout the book, I often gave you options. For example, within the universal principle that every business needs to have a KPI for employee engagement, there were a variety of items for your HR director to consider, things you and the director could choose from to make a set of six employee engagement metrics for themselves to blend into one single KPI, which would be the metric the HR director would share with the CEO. Once you have the principles under your belt, your coach's role is to observe, ask questions, and challenge you to think differently. Perhaps you've heard about some train wrecks other business owners have had with coaching. Those stories aren't false. The coaching industry is still a bit of a Wild West, and if you have colleagues whose businesses were damaged when they listened to a coach, the truth is that the problem is baked into the statement: "listened to a coach." The coach's job is to listen to you, not tell you what to do.

The biggest problem is when a coach gets impatient and tries to make a decision for you. A lot of business coaches are too nervous about proving results. They think that you have to execute on those KPIs within six weeks or they're going to be out of work. A good coach should be patient with you as you grow and should have the grit to wait it out. Change takes time.

You need to oversee the agenda. You need to make the choices about how your business is going to run. If you listen carefully to the disaster stories, the titanic failures other owners have had with their coaches, you'll likely notice a thread: the coach got impatient. The coach got frustrated. The coach thought someone should have made more progress, faster. The coach got caught up in "providing value" and forgot that the value of coaching isn't in what the coach does – it is in what the coach doesn't do.

A really good business coach will bring a patient, listening ear, respond to challenges with great principles to consider, and facilitate discussion where you and your team truly look at options you'd never considered before.

If you want someone to tell you what to do – that's a consultant's role. They don't just bring principles, they tell you how and when to apply those principles.

How To Select A Coach That's Right For You

If you interview several candidates for your CFO, COO, or CMO opening, why not do the same for your external executive/ leadership/ business coach? People say that you ought to have "chemistry" with your coach and that is true. However, there are a few other things to consider. Versatility and experience, sure. Trust is equally important.

One thing I recommend is that you get a coach **who does NOT know your industry.** This forces the coach to stay in the coaching role and allows you to stay in the expert role. That may sound counterintuitive, but the reality is that the best coaching comes from a place of not-knowing. The coach should be comfortable being the second-smartest person in the meeting. A good coaching mantra is "Stay Curious, My Friends." A coach who doesn't know your industry will have an easier time staying curious.

If you tend to be a down-to-business person, a "D" on the Disc® Personality Profile, get in and get out, you might consider getting a coach who's sort of the opposite, a fun-loving joker, an "I" on the Disc, someone who will challenge you to relax and remember that building a great culture is just as important as being productive.

If you tend to be a fun, charismatic person who feels comfortable with whatever happens, consider getting a coach who's going to nail you down on your action steps, who won't leave a meeting until everyone knows exactly what they're doing and when it's expected to be done.

A good coach should be both personable and tough, able to bring a balance of both, ready to challenge you to either lighten up your attitude and relax or tighten up your operations even to the extent of letting someone go if they're not suited to their position.

Finally, there's the obvious. How long has the coach been in business? And I don't mean "How long were they an executive in a company?" I mean, how long have they been in the business of coaching? Do they have coach-specific training? Do they have former clients who can give them a testimonial? (Watch out for testimonials that applaud the coach for all their "great advice".)

Where To Find A Coach

The coaching industry has been growing for about 30 years now, and while the coaching world is unregulated in the USA, it's still the Wild West out there. The industry has become somewhat more regulated in the European Union, with tighter laws around confidentiality and security for your personal information.

First, if you want a coach who is specifically trained in the World-Class Speed principles, you'll want to connect with a coach from Catipult.ai. At Catipult, we have solutions for every budget; one-on-one coaching, group coaching with a peer board, and as-needed coaching for businesses who purchase a license to our software.

If you want to try your hand at facilitating your own meetings, you can simply subscribe to the software and use our Catipult University to train yourself and your executive team on everything from the Six Core KPIs to how to use CHARP to update status on an action step.

Here's where you can go to ask for a few Catipult coaches to interview: www.catipult.ai.

If you've decided not to use a Catipult coach and want to find someone who has a great deal of training in coach-specific skill sets and has earned a credential from a globally recognized, third-party governing body, consider coaches who are certified by the International Coach Federation (ICF). They are accountable to their organization for ethical standards and competent practice.

If you want to become a member of a peer board of like-minded business owners that meets locally, look at Vistage®.

There are many ways to find a coach, and ensure the coach is the right fit. Don't rush to get a coach any faster than you would when hiring your next CFO.

How To Become A Catipult Coach

Catipult is always on the lookout for world-class business coaches who want to build their practice using the Catipult software with their clients and facilitating three-year outcomes and meetings. There is an application and training process in place for those interested. Some experience in business and training in coaching skills is a plus. To learn more about becoming a Catipult coach, visit Caipult.ai.

Industry Expert Interviews And Case Studies:

Geoff Hetherington

Bateau Bay, NSW Australia

I've been a business coach for the last 12 years, after 30-plus years as a C-suite executive in Southeast Asia and Australia, in 12 different industries. Before that, I was a visiting lecturer at universities on business, as well as being a C-suite executive concurrently. Even earlier, I was a high school teacher.

I'm a certified Business Continuity Planning expert; I'm one of 45 Certified Advisory Board Chairs here in Australia. So I run advisory boards. I'm also a Governance Board Chair as well. The point is, I've been around the block a few times, I'm T-Shaped: I'm a mile wide and a mile deep, my expertise runs across an awful lot of businesses, disciplines and industries. In the last 12 years, I've helped 180 businesses. No one has complained! No one has asked for their money back. So I figure that counts as being pretty successful. I'm talking about everyone – from someone who's starting a business in their garage to multinational corporations.

When I started business coaching, I would get people to come up with their personal goals and outcomes, then their business goals and outcomes. When most people do that, the two never meet up. I always taught them that your personal ones have to be supported by your business ones. I thought I was pretty much the only coach in the world doing that. And then I heard about this guy called Peter Fuller, who had this software which does exactly that. So, I got involved.

And Catipult is a great add-on. For me, it's an additive to my business. It's not the core of my business, but it's a fantastic tool for most businesses that I've come across. The key is to decide when to introduce it to them because there's quite a bit of preliminary foundational work to get in place first before you introduce them to Catipult. But once the foundations are solid, then it's the tool that helps take it to the next level.

Veterinarian Case Study

One of my clients has four veterinary practices. It's a multi-million-dollar business. In terms of staff numbers, there's probably 40 to 50 staff. There is a practice manager, a senior veterinary nurse and there's staff at each practice. And we put an operations manager into their business.

So it's reasonably substantial. It's certainly not the biggest veterinary group in the country, but it's a very nicely built one. The owner and his wife worked 10 years to build this thing up. Not long ago, they hired a new operations manager (against my advice - the role was needed, but the person hired was not a good fit) and lo and behold, six months later, they'd all but destroyed the business.

The owner had to roll up his sleeves and get things together. In Australia, the veterinary industry is incredibly thin on the ground in terms of good staff, whether they're vets or practice managers or veterinary nurses, which means that you have mediocre people getting paid good money and really good people often have a ridiculous expectation of how much they should get compensated. But they did have a group of employees who were pretty good and worked together. This operations manager came in and destroyed all that. So the owner is having to find new staff because a lot of people left, a lot of the people that were brought in by the operations manager were the wrong people, so they're moving them on. All in all, a disaster. I introduced them to Catipult as a means of starting to tie it all back together, particularly at the practice manager, senior vet, and senior nurse level. To me, KPIs are what the owner is accountable for, but the action steps are what people are responsible for.

We're still finalizing the setup, but we've already started using it and already people are getting on the same page, there's more of a cohesive feeling across the four practices that are operating at the moment. But more importantly, the practice managers are now stepping up because they've got very clear responsibilities and accountabilities, whereas before it was a bit wishy-washy. So that's good.

Q: What sorts of businesses do you think would *not* be a great fit for Catipult?

Smaller businesses: One of my clients is a world-famous physiotherapist, but he's in his 70's, his wife is in her late 60's, his hands are giving up on him, so I've started getting him to create some online courses and stuff like that. But there are only two of them working in the company. It really doesn't make a lot of sense to invest the money and time and effort into Catipult. I mean, why have a weekly 80-minute meeting designed by Catipult when they can just sit down at the breakfast table and check the to-do list? It just doesn't make sense.

There are certain businesses, like the hobby-type business, people who are selling stuff on Etsy or eBay shops, it's probably not the right thing for them. What it really comes down to is how good the coach is and how well developed the business is. I've got a current client who's in medical labeling. They save lives by producing accurate medical labels. I walked in and they were 70 percent under production capacity. We've now got that to 15 percent. Changed workflows, brought in folding machines, and so on. But they're getting to the stage where they're going to be the right size and have the right foundations for me to bring in Catipult and talk about how we can use it.

In a lot of family businesses, Catipult's not necessarily the right tool. If it's a husband and wife and they're wearing all the hats (which they shouldn't be), the time's not right for them. I'm working for a furniture removalist company (a.k.a. "relocation and storage services" in North America). Now they're using Catipult. They heard about it and got excited about it. But it's been a real slog getting them set up because they do everything themselves. They need to have an operations manager, but they haven't hired one, they need to have a couple of maintenance managers and a logistics manager, but they haven't hired them. We're setting Catipult up with that structure in mind but they're still owning everything. So it's not really fully effective for them just yet. There's an aspect to which there needs to be some kind of leadership team to use Catipult to maximum capacity and benefit.

I work with clients to get them out of the weeds and get them to what I call 'putting the business on cruise control,' so they can work on the business, not in it. And if they want to have three weeks off, they can go away and confidently come back and know the business is still running. In most cases, it runs better when the boss is away, to be honest. There needs to be that management layer. It is perfect for that type of traditional business setup.

Now, if it's a very flat structure, it can still work. But I don't think the utility of it is as great as if you've got the traditional pyramid. Unless you want to move from the flat to the pyramid, which is what I'm doing with the removalists, for instance, then yes. We're building the structure that they need to have for the future, and now we've got to get sufficient extra revenue coming in so I can start populating the structure.

The best use cases are where you've got a management team. If you've got a management team in a business, it's perfect. But pre-management team, it's okay if you're committed to working towards it. And if you don't have a management team and you don't ever want to have a management team, then you can use it, but I wouldn't recommend it.

INDUSTRY EXPERT INTERVIEWS AND CASE STUDIES:

A Conversation with Ben Wolfe, Fractional Integrator

Peter: Your company is the largest in the nation for this kind of thing. What's a fractional integrator and what got you into the business?

Ben: The main idea is that it's the conductor of your orchestra. You have a lot of instruments playing. You have marketing instruments, sales instruments, operations instruments, however you deliver your product or service, finance instruments, HR instruments, all the pieces of the business.

Whatever the business owner does; business development, big relationships, Research & Development, whatever it happens to be, is like the first chair violinist. And the integrator is the conductor of the orchestra. The conductor doesn't play an instrument, which is especially true of the fractional integrator. Very often a full-time integrator will also 'play an instrument.' They may sit in some operational seat and function as the integrator, as the conductor of all the seats, all the main functions of the business: marketing, sales, operations, finance, technology, or HR.

Because the fractional integrator is fractional, they're not playing an instrument in the orchestra, but without a conductor, there would be no tempo. People would not be playing the same piece of music at the same rhythm, and it would sound horrible. It would not be an effective orchestra. The integrator takes everything that's going on in the visionary's head now and into the future, in all the departments and skill sets of all the individual leaders, and sets a rhythm or a cadence and makes sure that everybody's playing the same piece of music, working together. And then you can actually have a symphony. When you play without a conductor, there's no symphony.

When they're smaller, the owner can cover it with just sheer force of will. Up to a certain point, that works.

You probably even need to have that to be maximally agile and be successful and survive the startup gauntlet. But at some point in your growth, it just stops working, whether that comes when you're at 20 people or 50 people or 100 people. And that's when you need a good integrator.

A fractional integrator is somebody who's run or owned businesses like this before. It's not their first rodeo. They're able to marry their experience to the unique situation and product and team and customers and vision of whatever business they're working with. They make sense of the current chaos and everything that will be going on and might be going on and all the potential hundred priorities that are vying for what should be done first, and you feel like you want them all done yesterday... and they put together a roadmap.

That's what a lot of our firm focuses on at the beginning, figuring out what's the roadmap: we ask the question, "What do we do first, second, and third, to harness our limited energy that's available for making change?"

You have a lot of energy that's going towards running the day-to-day. And how do we channel the limited energy that's left for making change into a way that's going to honor the day-to-day? You can't uproot what's already been built and what's already working, but simultaneously, you have to do the things that need to be put into place or fixed to really scale this thing up and make it to the next level. That is what people want to do when they bring in the fractional integrator.

Peter: How does that differ from a Chief Operating Officer (COO)? Have you worked in situations where they had a chief operating officer, director of operations? How do the two work together? Do you only bring in a fractional integrator when there isn't an operations person?

Ben: Well, it's important to make a distinction, I think, between a director of operations and an integrator or COO. So, I'm defining those two terms very differently. In some places they even call that a COO, (which makes our conversation even more confusing,) but when I see VP of Ops or Head of Operations, that tells me that person oversees the day-to-day delivery of the product or service that is the core of the business. That's what the VP of Ops does, right? They build the products, deliver the products, provide the service, they're in charge of that, whatever that is. If it's a law firm, it's legal services. If it's making widgets, it's the production and distribution of widgets. That's what the VP of Ops does. They're not in charge of marketing, they're not in charge of sales, they're not in charge of finance, they're not in charge of HR, they're not in charge of internal administration.

You do need to have somebody in that role as well, because when the integrator comes in on a fractional basis, if you have 10 trucks out there delivering HVAC services at homes, you can't have a fractional integrator managing those 10 drivers. It's important that you have a head of ops in place. Even if it's the owner sitting in that role as an additional seat, even though they wish it wasn't, it's critical that there's somebody in that role.

Conversely, an integrator or COO is the person who leads the leadership team. They lead whoever's responsible for marketing, sales, finance, operations, technology, HR, whatever other leadership functions there are.

179

They manage the entire business through those leaders, through whoever's responsible for those different departments. They manage the head of operations, too.

Peter: And how does that differ from an implementer or a coach?

Ben: The biggest difference is that a coach or integrator is not responsible for execution of the plan that they helped the person come up with. They are responsible to help people get clarity on making key decisions, maybe teaching and giving people tools that they need to operate their business, but they're not operating their business. They teach the tools. They facilitate all your decision-making and help you apply those tools to your business. They are an outsider who observes and helps you see things about yourself and about your decision making that you have become blind to. *But what they're not responsible for* is to actually implement the things that they just taught you. A coach is sitting on the outside of your accountability chart or outside of your organizational chart. But the Integrator or COO are on your organizational chart. They may be filling that role on a fractional or full-time basis, but the role itself is no different. They don't have all the baggage and prejudices of everything that you've gone through until now, so they have the benefits of that outsider, but they're also on your organizational accountability chart. They're on your team. They're not just coaching your team as an outsider.

Peter: In your experience, how do executive teams respond when the CEO brings in a fractional integrator? Do you get any pushback from the executive team members? What case studies do you have there?

Ben: There's some pushback sometimes, people are hesitant about it. One of the things that I think is most surprising though, and people don't expect this, but a lot of times these members of the team open up to the integrator extraordinarily quickly, because what the business owner and maybe even the people themselves aren't aware of before they get into this relationship with the COO or integrator, is that there may be a lot of frustration built up over years. There are issues they've been pointing out, and nothing changes, things get swept under the rug. Or they're getting frustrated with the whiplash they get from doing this, doing that, then doing the third thing. Another situation we'll see is that they've noticed very few things ever reach completion.

Suddenly they have an experienced business leader who has the ear of the visionary, or the founder, and they come in and they want to know what you think. They want to know what you're seeing. They want to know what's working. They want to know what's not working. And the employees and leadership team suddenly realize, "Oh my gosh, I have an ally here." When that happens, there's almost a vomiting of all the dirty laundry, about the visionary or the owner and about their colleagues, you know? And so, you get a lot of good stuff to sort through!

I've begun engagements with clients like that. Even the most difficult people are just very open right at the beginning. They're not just like sitting there with their hands folded in front of them, like, "Why should I talk to you? What, are you the next big-shot consultant? I know you're going to fire everybody." We just show people that we're listening to them and taking their feedback seriously. Then they see that you can be an advocate for them. So, if they say something in the leadership team meeting and you back them up, they say, "Oh, finally, I'm not screaming into the wind here. I have somebody who's championing some of the things that I've been saying."

I had a call yesterday with a member of my team who is starting with a new client today. He's coming in as their fractional integrator. I had a call yesterday with the visionary and his former integrator, who was the integrator until yesterday. I listened, and there's definitely some resistance. But when we acknowledge that all they want is what's best for the business, we show that we're really listening, we don't steamroll over anybody, and show respect: Usually, people open up very quickly.

Peter: I've had some CEOs that were really into the idea of getting help, but they weren't into changing themselves. Therefore, the organization ran like a chicken with its head cut off. What sort of examples do you have of CEOs who are not the best fit for this? And what could a CEO do to make sure he is the best fit for it?

Ben: I'll tell you about one client that we dropped recently. It was a professional services company, and the head partner said all the right things, like this: "We came to you because we wanted to get better, and to delegate, and I want to free myself up, and not be so underwater all the time, and always be the bottleneck for every decision…"

My team member went in, and for the first few months, that was one of her favorite clients. She looked at what's going on, helped them set up the right processes, the right systems of accountability that would give the opportunity for the partners and associates to have a lot more independent action.

But we realized over time that the leader didn't want to let go of anything. Nothing was able to change. He tried to put the building blocks into place so that he could let go, so that he could do the things he said he wanted to do, but he wouldn't let go of any of the work. We tried to address it one way, tried to address it with him another way. There was always some objection. We tried to address those. But at some point, you've got to take a leap of faith. Finally, we had a come-to-Jesus conversation with the guy. I said, "I don't want to just take your money. My goal is to deliver a self-managing business. I'm trying to lay out a path here, but you're not walking down it. I'm not here to get paid to do nothing. So, this engagement will only be able to be successful if you're able and willing to go down this path." We agreed upon some action plans for another month, but it didn't change. Finally, we just gave our 30-day notice. I said, "Sorry. I don't think we can help, so over the next thirty days, we'll help you transition out, so you'll know what to do, how to continue the work that we've begun, if you choose to."

You can lead a horse to water, but you can't make him drink. It's true that people need to let go of the vine, people need to delegate. And it's also true that if you don't have the right people in the right seats, then you really can't delegate because it won't get done right. If you let go of the wheel, it will go off the rails, the car will drive off the highway. But if you've got the right people in the right seats, and there are guidelines for whatever kind of action that people need to take in their roles, then it's on the visionary or the business owner if they're not willing to let go.

Peter: One of the biggest challenges I've seen is the open-door policy, where a business owner just can't close the door and delegate conversations to somebody else, because they started the company, and everybody has always come to them. Even when they're adding a management layer, they still think it's cool to have an open-door policy. Well, that leads to somebody coming up to them and asking them to make a decision. Oftentimes they do, even though it should be the decision of their VP or their operations person. How do you advise CEOs to put down that ego addiction? They're so used to being needed constantly for everything. And now they've got to make this move to scale and get bigger.

Ben: I think the message there is to recognize that you're not helping the people whose questions you're answering when you have that open door policy. Instead, you're debilitating them. I know the owner is answering the questions because he or she cares about them and loves them and wants to be there for them, those are the motivating feelings. But instead, they're making them unable to make their own decisions. It can begin to change if every time someone asks you a question, if you ask them questions in return, like, "What would you do?" Or "What does the handbook say?" Or "What does the process document tell you to do in this situation?"

At first, you get the answer, "I'm not sure."

You can respond by saying, "OK, look it up and then let me know if you have any follow-up questions, or talk to your manager." Don't let them get off that easily. It's the same problem with managers. It's not just the owners. That's what I call the problem of 'helicopter management', when you have the wrong people or even the right people sitting in the wrong seats, or you have bad processes or processes that were just added to over and over, never reviewed or revised, which creates this Frankenstein-like collection of things that have built up over time. When you have that open door policy, or when the manager reviews every proposal before it goes out, or inspects every widget before it gets delivered, or there's three levels of checks on everything that gets done, then you have either bad processes or the wrong people.

Often the owners never suffer very much from the consequences of having the wrong people in the wrong seats or wrong processes because they have enough babysitting and hovering and managing going on that they mask it. They end up with a 5 percent profit instead of a 15 percent profit, because they get all these extra people, waste, inefficiency, and bad morale because of the people issues that they're not addressing. So, the pain is anesthetized because the results aren't that bad and because everything's being masked by all these too-available managers or owners.

You need to manage based on outcomes and KPIs. And that's what Catipult is all about: your measurables and KPIs. If a salesperson is responsible for X number of outgoing outreaches, or X number of proposal calls, or X numbers of proposals sent, or X number of deals closed, and they've got four or five numbers that they're responsible for, you can manage to the numbers. Or rather, you *don't have to hover* and ask them about their calls that day. You have numbers, you can just wait till your weekly review, find out if they are on track or off track, and take those numbers and the requirements and the minimums or maximums seriously.

Peter: Why wouldn't somebody want at least a fractional COO when there's a lot of value in bringing one on, even if you do have the head of operations position covered?

Ben: Here's a couple of times where you're not going to want a fractional COO: one is a very simple situation where you have a business and a leadership team that is very non-tech savvy, maybe a very blue-collar business, maybe people grew up in the business, or elevated through the ranks of the business, any team who are not comfortable with technology: If they are unable to find the right fit for a fractional COO or integrator who is local and can work with them in person, there would be so much friction trying to make some kind of remote engagement work with a particular leadership team that is just not going to be practical.

Another example is if the owner thinks that nobody knows as much as he or she does.

Third, you have a case of what I've heard called 'terminal uniqueness,' which is a mentality owners can get where they think everything about your business, everything about your team, everything about your customers, and everything about your product or service is unique. It's not like any of your competitors. It's not like anybody else out there. Nothing that works for anybody else is likely to work for you and or your business. There are a lot of people who think that way. Most of the time they're wrong. I'm sure there's some minority where they're right, but most of the time they're not. 80 to 90 percent of the things in the business are really the same as many other people.

If the owner doesn't have the ability to see somebody with experience, who's done it before at businesses as big or bigger than his, and grown businesses like hers before, if the owner can't see them as having much to add, then they won't be able to. It would be a self-fulfilling prophecy. It would not go well.

I've had discovery calls where the business owner spends the whole time telling me how great their team is, and how great their product is, and how great their service is and how great they are and how great the team is (again) and how great their processes and systems are. On and on. I ask them, "Okay, so why are we on the phone today? Why are we talking? Sounds like things are pretty good."

"Well, we could use some little tweaks, you know, nobody's perfect."

And if that's the way they're talking, you can just tell it's not going to work.

Don't bother hiring a fractional integrator if that's how you feel, or a fractional COO, or almost anybody else who is not just an order taker, because they're not going to be able to justify whatever they're charging!

If the owner is not going to see the value in it, or listen to what they recommend, they're not going to be able to add very much value. It would not be a good use of the company's resources.

Hiring Great Leaders Who Are Hungry For Accountability: A Conversation With Alec Broadfoot, CEO, VisionSpark

Alec Broadfoot is the CEO of VisionSpark, (www.visionsparksearch.com) one of Catipult's newest partners. They support owners and entrepreneurs by recruiting great leaders who are the right fit for the company, and they use scientific hiring methods to attain a 95 percent hiring rate (against an industry average of 60 percent).

Because Employees and Leadership are two of the Seven Business Drivers, and getting the right people in the right seats is critical to success with Catipult or with KPIs in general, Alec agreed to chat with me about some of the challenges of what it takes to find the right hire. Here are some snippets from our conversation.

Alec: My vision is to help entrepreneurs free up their time and to remove stress from life by hiring the right leaders. Often visionaries, myself included, tend to under-hire. We tend to hire from a budget standpoint, and that means we aren't thinking big enough. I'll usually challenge my clients to think bigger. They never come to me and say, "Man, my profit's down because I spent all that money." They never say that. They're thankful that their quality of life is better and their business is running better. That's my primary vision; and my secondary vision is to have an amazing culture for my team. Some of my employees teared up when they told me that VisionSpark is the best place they've ever worked. I want to create a great work environment for them; a great career for them and see them grow.

Peter: So what do you feel is the bridge between an accountability system and culture? In general, what would you say your experience has taught you, by working directly with companies that have an accountability structure in place, compared to companies that haven't implemented a system, and how that impacts culture?

Alec: It's important that everybody has some sort of metric that they're held accountable to. You can't manage what you can't measure. We've all heard that expression. One of my favorite two-by-twos is from Jack Welch where you have the high performers in the top right corner, they fit your core values. Then you have the puppies in the top left, they have your core values, they're not yet top performers. In the bottom right, you have your terrorists. Those are the great performers, but they do not play well in the sandbox with others. And then in the bottom corner, you have the 'rats', because it's the opposite of 'star'. And they have neither your core values, nor do they perform. Visionaries are not very good at figuring out who the rats are because when you flip on the lights, the rats act busy, and they try to look like they are stars. As soon as you leave the room they start complaining and gossiping... but when they have a number, a target, something they're accountable to, they're going to self-select, in or out, right? They can't hide, so they'll leave. That's why accountability is so important.

Having the right leaders in place is more important than ever. It's well documented that people don't leave jobs: they leave their managers or bosses. You want leaders who love to coach and mentor others, who make sure that individuals have what they need to do their job well, who are attentive.

Peter: That's exactly what KPIs do. We often run into situations where that mirror is so powerful, that when it shows what people are supposed to be doing and proves the fact they're not doing it, even on the activity layer— people have practically run right out of the building. The rats don't like the light. You'll find people on the executive team who become passive-aggressive. They don't want to do it. They say they can't do it. I ran into a VP of sales who had lots of experience in the industry. You'd think he would be better than this, but he just started griping and moaning and saying, "Things aren't fair." I mean, he turned into a little kid.

The irony was that the only thing the CEO did was put some metrics into Catipult: they were the metrics that the VP of sales had developed himself. They began to have a Monday meeting to go through those metrics. It wasn't like a performance improvement plan or anything. The CEO said, "This is what we need to do. And we're going to do it. So what are the action items you're taking to hit your own metrics?" The VP of Sales got squeamish. I've seen that behavior over and over. That's the rats. It seemed like he was okay before, as far as his attitude went, but he wasn't really performing as he could have been. As soon as Catipult was there to hold him accountable we uncovered something we didn't expect. That's what Catipult does, in a nutshell.

Alec: Sometimes a good CEO will push them out and hire somebody who is on the right train. Other CEOs really have a hard time with it: they bend to the pressure and water things down because that person happened to be with them for 10 years or started the business with them, or they're related.

What you're talking about, Peter, is a *culture* of accountability. I would say it starts with the leader, making sure you have the right leaders in place. And these leaders need to be people-oriented leaders, good at coaching, mentoring, encouraging, focusing on strengths, and removing obstacles. They need to communicate how they're going to hold their direct reports accountable. How is their performance going to be measured? What does success look like? That needs to be done on day one. Next, they need to hire the right people. Individuals in an organization who don't have the core values or don't want to be held accountable will self-select out. They need to hire people who want to be accountable. It's important to communicate that beginning with the job ad, through the interview and assessments. I use an assessment that I think is the best one out there specifically for hiring. It starts with the hiring process, but it doesn't stop there. There needs to be successful onboarding. And that's where you reiterate how the new hire is going to be held accountable. A year from now, this is what's expected. This is what I expect in 180 days, 90 days, 30 days. Gallup has a Q12 survey which poses the question, "Do you have the equipment you need to do your job successfully?" That's something a lot of employers don't focus on.

About fifteen years ago I met with one of the largest McDonald's franchisees in the country. I was teasing him about the high turnover rate that McDonald's has. He said, "Alec, my turnover is the lowest in the country."

I said, "Really? You're probably paying above market."

"Nope," he said, "I'm paying right at market rates. But when that cash register is broken, I fix it. When that fryer is broken, I fix it. I have soft mats on the floor so they're comfortable at work. I make sure they can do their job well, because people leave when they don't have the equipment to do their job well."

Peter: Steve Jobs says a small group of A-plus players can run circles around large groups of B and C players. I used to do a lot of speaking around the country at Vistage groups. I would ask the Vistage members, "How much more productive are your A players?" And I would get answers anywhere from 20 percent more, all the way up to 20 times more productive.

"Great," I'd say, "let's just settle somewhere in between, like 50 percent more productive. How much more are you paying your A players versus your B players?" The answer was usually in the range of two to five percent more. So I developed a little tool to show how if you hire A players and you pay them more, you can actually be more productive and have higher profitability. You want to hire A players; so don't be afraid to pay them a little bit more, because you're going to get tons of return.

It reminds me of a story someone told me about his grandfather, who was an VP of engineering back in the 1970s and 80s with a company called Gifford-Hill Concrete. He was working in Texas when the union went on strike in California. So, the company sent about twenty salaried employees, engineers, and flew them out to California to run the concrete plant, which was typically run by 200 union employees. Within two or three weeks, the salaried skeleton crew was getting more productivity out of that plant than the 200 union guys had been doing before they went on strike. There were no scabs, just experienced concrete executives running machines (and fixing them, because they were engineers, and they knew how to fix stuff and didn't complain about it not being their job to fix stuff). That was the end of the strike.

Now, I want to get back to recruiting. What do you look for in candidates when you're recruiting people for structure-based companies like this? And how do you help business owners find the right person, so they don't end up with somebody like that VP of sales that I described?

Alec: Well, it starts with really good behavioral interviewing and using assessments. There's so much that we can tell from that. The average company, when they're interviewing, has a 17 percent chance of predicting someone's future success. By adding a high-quality assessment, you more than triple those odds, to 53 percent success rate. Just having a high-quality assessment is going to help tremendously.

Next, let's talk about interviewing. I teach my clients to use the phrase, "Tell me about a time when…"

We might start with something like, "Would you describe yourself as someone who is easily held accountable?" It's a yes or no question. But you would follow that up by asking, "Tell me about a time when you worked for someone, and they were really clear in what was expected of you right from the start." And then you can take that further: "Tell me about a time when you really had a hard time meeting performance expectations." When you turn it and you make it negative, then you see who they are. They may say, "You know what, I've never been like that. I'm always someone to do… X, Y, and Z." But what do you get if they're honest? Here's an example: "I worked for a manager in a restaurant. It was one of my first jobs, and he was not happy. I was calling in sick, I had tennis practice, and I had a really hard time." You can really find out who that person is. That phrase, "Tell me about a time," is key. You need to listen for specific examples.

When we interview for positions, the candidates get rated in 12 areas. We use a behavior-based interview, on which they get scored. If they don't have the right answers, they don't move forward in the process. We not only have the right questions, but we also know the answers we're looking for. I'll give you an example. One question we ask is, "A manager achieves many things in the performance of his or her duties. What accomplishments give you the greatest satisfaction?" Over half the time we get the wrong answer. "My greatest accomplishment was when I was in Sacramento. I took over an operation that was failing and I turned it around and it became 10 percent profitable within a year." Or we might get, "My greatest accomplishment was when we grew this business from $10 million in sales to $15 million," or whatever. *That's the wrong answer.* The right answer revolves around the growth of others, seeing others succeed, building others. "My greatest accomplishment is when my employee Joanne had this huge desire to learn. I spent three years developing her and now she's a VP of XYZ company. That is my greatest accomplishment." Those are the right answers. We score the answers, and more often than not, our clients pick the candidates that have the best scores.

Peter: You told me about a time when it wasn't a good fit, when the guy said he wanted a CFO by Friday... Tell us about a time when it was a great fit.

Alec: We had a client located in the middle of a cornfield. They were in the agricultural business, literally in the middle of a cornfield. They said, "We need a materials manager. We heard that you could help us with that."

I asked them to tell me about the company culture and followed that up by asking whether this was going to be for a new position or a replacement.

The other person went quiet for a moment before they said, "Actually it's a replacement. We thought our guy was going to be great. We painted their office for them and everything. But they only stayed for four days."

They were only a couple hours' drive from Columbus, so I drove up there and found this old plant – it hadn't been renovated in 50 years. I said, "Well, take me to the office. Where's this new hire going to work?" This office had a super tiny window. It looked out on a metal hallway connecting two big plants on either side. The inside of the office was freshly painted – a gray cement color – and I said, "This isn't an office. This is a jail cell."

But after asking some more questions, I realized they didn't need someone who was going to enjoy this jail cell of an office. The employee would have to be out and about, on the plant floor, looking for areas where more training was needed, bottlenecks and obstacles, and seeing how they could help. We were hired to find someone who would fit the role. That was nine or ten years ago now, and that person's still there. So, that's an example of a position that we helped fill in a very difficult situation.

Peter: Thanks, Alec, really great stories, I've appreciated talking with you!

GRATITUDE AND ACKNOWLEDGEMENTS

Many thanks to the members of our fantastic team at Catipult ... who are acting toward hitting all their personal and business outcomes and KPIs. Your work makes it possible for us to impact the world together, and we're doing that in some amazing ways, as business owners and thousands of their employees find themselves reinvigorated and realigned, and on a path to that three-year outcome of being World-Class. It's an honor to work alongside each one of you.

Thanks to all the business clients I worked with during my time as a Vistage chair and ever since; Catipult was not created in a vacuum. Without your input on everything from which KPIs were most meaningful, useful, and relevant; to how you rated how well your meetings were run; and even to the CHARP language, we would not have the proven, world-class theory backing the superior software that we have today. We continue to evolve toward excellence every day, together.

Many independent coaches have given their time to being interviewed and offering their write-ups, graciously contributing their case studies so that this book could come alive with rich, recent, and relevant anecdotes. Thanks to each of you.

Thanks also to the many other coaches who are or soon will be our biggest advocates in the marketplace, inviting more and more business owners to become World-Class leaders of World-Class companies.

Thanks to Adam G. Fleming and his team at Victory Vision Publishing for their editorial work on this project.

Special thanks to Ken Thieneman, Derrick Christy, and Cathy Langham, whose companies incubated and kicked the tires on the software solution.

Last, but certainly not least is Sam Smith, CEO of RCRE, the largest privately held commercial real estate company in Indianapolis. He said, "Peter, we love your process and hate your spreadsheets. Here's $30,000 to start a software company." Thanks Sam. Your vision helped launch this entire system.

Thanks to Maia Siprashvili for tirelessly editing this book and living it every day. This book also couldn't have happened without the support of my family, Alyssa, Annie, Nick, and Nika.

GLOSSARY

Action Items: Projects or initiatives that must be done within a quarter or at the end of a quarter.

Cascading KPIs: KPIs at Level 2, 3, or lower, that support KPIs above. The idea is that all other KPIs should be connected to the six top level KPIs that the CEO or owner will see.

Catipult: 1) A coaching company. 2) A proprietary A.I. software with a dashboard for tracking Six Core KPIs in connection with The Seven Business Drivers™.

CHARP: A system for communicating progress on KPIs and Action items, using the five words Change, Help, Aware, Redirect, and Plan.

Churn: Ratio of new customers to lost customers. World-Class businesses look at Revenue Churn: new revenue to lost revenue.

Coaching: A future-oriented, non-directive process where the client sets the agenda.

Concentration of Revenue from One Customer: The percentage of a company's revenue derived from their single largest customer. A World-Class Concentration of Revenue is under 20 percent.

Discussions: Not problems. Not issues. Not challenges. Discussions are just that: two or three people in a room talking about something that has come up. Use the word "discussion" to steer away from negativity.

EBITDA: Earnings Before Interest, Tax, Depreciation and Amortization

Efficiency: Organizing for speed.

Employee Engagement Score: An indicator of employee satisfaction taking into account a variety of factors including pay, opportunities for advancement, balance, culture and other intangibles.

Growth, World-Class: Growth at 5 percent or more above industry growth rate against previous year or same month or quarter in previous year.

KPI: Key Performance Indicator. A measure of how a company is performing in relation to their Three-Year Outcome.

Meetings, World-Class: Focused on KPIs and other metrics, world-class meetings are facilitated to be only as long as they need to be, and to only involve the people who need to be there.

Pipeline: Sales quota divided by close rate

Reticular activating system: A center in the brain which controls a broad spectrum of brain activity including consciousness.

Rhythm: Meeting sequences that allow the company to stay on track with KPIs, including the Weekly 80, Six-Week Tactical, and Quarterly Strategic meetings.

Rockefeller Habits: Ten disciplines to cultivate that create clear communication and build positive culture within a business or organization.

Start with You: The concept that a business owner needs to have personal outcomes equal in importance with his or her business outcomes. See the book *Start with You* by Peter Fuller.

Three-year outcome statement: A statement for personal, professional and business growth, designed to fool the reticular activating system into believing the job is already done, the statement begins with "The year is ___ and I am ___."

World-Class: Operating on a certain set of structures and metrics that give you the ability to be above (or below, when below is better) than average in most, if not all, areas.

ENDNOTES

1   https://fortune.com/2023/09/12/boeing-executives-david-calhoun-brian-west-return-to-office-relocation/

2   The Rockefeller Habits are based on the principles of John D. Rockefeller as described by Verne Harnish in *Scaling Up at https://ScalingUp.com*

3   "United Breaks Guitars: The power of one voice in the age of social media" by Dave Carroll.

4   Zaffron, Steve and David Logan, *The Three Laws of Performance*: *Rewriting the Future of Your Organization and Your Life*. (San Francisco: Josse Bass, 2009), 6.

5   https://www.boeing.com/principles/values.page

6   https://www.netjets.com/en-us/company-culture

7   https://www.youtube.com/watch?v=ACZhpCdfEdY

8   https://www.forbes.com/sites/qai/2022/12/11/elon-musks-six-rules-would-you-survive-working-for-elon-musk/

9   https://www.emyth.com/

10 https://www.statista.com/statistics/1373870/top-nonprofits-ceo-compensation-us/

11 https://www.maddyness.com/uk/2020/12/30/adapt-to-survive-interview-with-ross-thornley-ceo-aqai/

ABOUT THE AUTHOR

Peter C. Fuller, the founder of Catipult. AI, a technology and coaching company, emphasizes a metric-based approach to strategic planning. This approach not only saves time but also enhances valuation and drives profitability. Fuller is also an accomplished author with two books under his belt: "World-Class Speed" and "Start with You". His newsletter, "The KPI Guy", boasts a readership of over 16,000 business owners and executives weekly. Before delving into the realm of metrics, Fuller served as an adjunct professor of entrepreneurship at Purdue University and played pivotal roles in the founding of six companies and two industry associations. When he's not immersed in his work, Fuller enjoys cycling, traveling, reading, participating in F45 workouts, and cherishing moments with his family. Additionally, he dedicates Wednesdays to assisting the homeless. For more information, you can visit his website at: *PeterCFuller.com*, or simply scan the QR code below.

Connect with Peter at Linkedin.com/in/petercfuller

CATIPULT AI

Throughout the course of this book, I have referred to Catipult multiple times, so it makes sense to give you a brief introduction.

Catipult is a software solution for business owners and CEOs to use to ensure that nothing in their business is done if it is not related to a Key Performance Indicator (KPI). It's designed to eliminate waste, particularly time wasted in meetings and time wasted pursuing things that have nothing to do with the business' core values, vision, mission, and three-year outcomes, and even saves time wasted in tracking too many KPIs in a clunky spreadsheet. It's designed to give your company world-class speed and efficiency, and assist you in creating great rhythms, too.

Catipult functions as a tracking dashboard, allowing users to track KPIs through our trademarked "Seven Business Drivers" and to check in on them with your team when appropriate – and only when appropriate – meaning it allows users to break the habit of micromanaging. Users begin by inputting some basic data about their business, like what industry they are in and some of their current financials, also including their three year outcome statements, beginning with a future-oriented statement like "The year is _____ and I am..." or "The year is _____ and our business is ..." Catipult's artificial intelligence reads the outcome statement and pre-programs suggested Key Performance Indicators. Everything Catipult does is geared toward those three-year outcomes, which are virtually guaranteed when we *focus on the right things* in business, the top six most important KPIs for every business, which we discussed in chapter four.

Catipult is fully customizable to user preferences and is designed to work for enterprise level companies but could be used by small companies as well.

As a company, Catipult also offers a variety of coaching solutions, from as-needed engagements with a certified Catipult coach to our signature Razor™ program, where a coach helps the owner or CEO not only set up the system in just a few weeks with a front-end heavy engagement, but also facilitates tactical meetings for the leadership team.

Therefore, Catipult is many things: A company. Intelligent software. A group of certified coaches who can function as your pilot. For the business owner, Catipult equates to a lifestyle built around World-Class Speed. Catipult is the private jet of KPI tracking solutions.

Normally, when we refer to Catipult throughout the book, we're talking about the software's dashboard.

I encourage you to play around with the software as you read through the book, (or go through it a second time) because then, you'll get more than a book... you'll get an experience. Catipult can be downloaded for free for your first month, at www.catipult.ai. Yes, that's *Catipult* with an I. *We know it's misspelled!*

This book comes to life in our software and with a meeting for a strategic assessment. You owe it to yourself, your family, and your employees to take advantage of this opportunity. To start your free assessment with one of our coaches, please scan the QR code below. Our coaches are former and/or current business owners with a high level of expertise in running organizations. They'll use the software to review not only the core metrics but also the other key strategic metrics for your industry and benchmark your company's performance against the targets the system creates. It is the fastest and most unique assessment you'll likely ever take.

Made in United States
North Haven, CT
06 July 2024

54476251R00122